The Seed of Wisdom

The Seed of Wisdom
The Meaning of Reality

John Hopkins

Compton Press . Salisbury

Copyright © J. Hopkins 1972

First published in Great Britain by
The Compton Press Ltd.,
Compton Chamberlayne, Salisbury, Wiltshire,
in association with J. Hopkins.
SBN 9001 9317 4

Designed and printed in England at the
Compton Press.

Contents

Author's Note 1

Introduction 5

1 The Constitution of Man 11

2 The Etheric Body 18

3 Energy Centres and the Endocrine Glands 25

4 The Soul and the Doctrine of Re-birth 36

5 On Evolution 47

6 The World of Energies 56

7 The Seven Rays 65

8 On Meditation 80

9 Practical Application 93

Conclusion 108

Appendixes 114

Author's Note

THE AGELESS WISDOM teaching has been handed down to us over the centuries by word of mouth through the 'guru-chela', or Master-disciple, relationship, mainly in the Orient. In the Occident, the more esoteric aspects of religion have come to our knowledge through the writings of the Saints and mystics, but also through lesser known channels of spiritual communication that may be more easily comprehended as we look at the teaching itself.

The most comprehensive and scientific approach to the subject was given out between the years 1875 and 1949, first through the writings of H. P. Blavatsky under the title of The Secret Doctrine and later, between 1919 and 1949, in a remarkable series of books by Alice A. Bailey written in telepathic communication with a Master of the Wisdom, Djwal Khul, often referred to as The Tibetan – or simply D. K.

These teachings are contained in some twenty books, dealing with the many aspects of the vast subject, some of which number over 700 pages, whilst one of them extends to 1300! Some of them are very much

The Seed of Wisdom

easier to follow than others which require a depth of intuitional enlightenment possessed by very few intellectuals or mystics alive today. Nevertheless, every one of these books can contribute ideas and ideals within the grasp of the man who has reached the stage of searching for a deeper meaning to life than appears on the surface. A list of these books is given in Appendix II; and in Appendix I will be found a statement by The Tibetan which fully explains his position in relation to the teaching.

The purpose of this booklet is to serve as an introduction to the subject of esotericism in general, but with particular reference to the Ageless Wisdom teaching as expounded by The Tibetan. It is in no sense whatever an attempt to teach, because, not only would this be presumptuous, it would actually debase the teaching. Each and every student of esotericism must find his own way along the path that leads to understanding, and each must interpret the teaching according to his ever increasing degree of spiritual awareness. My purpose therefore, I repeat, is not to teach, but to try and explain in so far as this is possible, and in relatively simple language, what the Ageless Wisdom teaching is all about.

During a period of over twenty years, reading and studying these books which for me carry utter conviction, with the invaluable help and guidance of the Arcane School, the phraseology of the books has inevitably impregnated my own mode of expression in

Author's Note

these matters. For this I make no apology; I only wish to acknowledge this to be the case, and to express my gratitude.

I quote extensively from the books of A. A. B. because so often any attempt to express the teaching in other words would only devalue the meaning. Under these circumstances, it would, I think, have been tedious to prefix these quotations in every case with repeated references to their source. Therefore I have not done so, and it can be assumed that, except where otherwise stated, all quotations are from the teachings as given in Alice Bailey's books.

Introduction

THIS SMALL book is about esotericism and the mysterious, invisible world of energies and thought-forms which underlies and is the real cause of all phenomena and all that happens in our lives, and in the lives to come, in this world, and in those other worlds of which we are insensible. It deals with things of the spirit, but not with spiritualism which is quite a different aspect of the subject.

Esotericism, according to the dictionary, pertains to doctrines taught privately, and relates to that which is hidden. But the doctrines are hidden, not because they are secret, but because our finite minds lack the state of consciousness that can penetrate into the infinite and beyond the world as it appears to our normal senses.

Esotericism is not a substitute for religion, but rather does it give deeper meaning to the orthodox teachings in that it is concerned with those spiritual energies which are the very basis of all religions. But when we attempt to penetrate into this world of energies, we find that spiritual knowledge is really no more than belief. Dr. Raynor Johnson, for many years

The Seed of Wisdom

Master of Queen's College, University of Melbourne, in his book The Situation of Modern Man, writes:

> All things of the Spirit exist intrinsically on a higher significant level than that to which intellect has access. The awareness which we may have of spiritual things is not intellectual, but rather a total knowing or mystical awareness in which, for a moment, the knower and the known have been one. It is almost as though knowledge, and particularly

spiritual knowledge, were arranged in layers; and in order to contact a higher layer we, or some part of our mental complex, has to become associated with that level of knowledge through an expansion of our normal state of awareness. This expansion of consciousness is a prerequisite for a deeper understanding of that outer manifestation of belief that we call religion. This is brought home to us very clearly in a definition of the religion of the future by the Tibetan Master, Djwal Khul:

> Recognition by the part of its relation to the whole, plus a constantly growing awareness of that relation.

If we attempt to rely on the intellect alone in our search for spiritual knowledge, we find that the analytical nature of the mind will cause us to see things as though they were separate. Although the knowledge will still be useful, it will be distorted by lack of

Introduction

recognition of the interdependence between the many parts and the Whole.

Esotericism basically is concerned with the understanding and use of the energies that condition our planet and all things existing in and on it. This understanding, or state of awareness, is really a state of being, in which a man can live his normal life with access to knowledge that can make its purpose increasingly more meaningful. But to accomplish this state of being, much more than spiritual knowledge is required, for knowledge is only a means to an end; and the end is wisdom.

Aptly enough, the dictionary defines wisdom as the application of knowledge to the best ends; and thus knowledge is the seed of wisdom. The Tibetan has described spiritual knowledge as:

> the awareness of requirements, and the ability to bring together the need and that which is required to meet that need.

If we interpret this as meaning an awareness of the needs of humanity and a recognition of what is required of us to meet those needs we discover the whole purpose of our lives, which is intended to be the expression of love and wisdom, in so far as this may be possible. And this is precisely what the Ageless Wisdom teaching is all about; ageless because it is as old as time itself, and also because it is for ever being

The Seed of Wisdom

renewed as man becomes more responsive to the source of the teaching.

But what, we may ask, *is* the source of this teaching? This question presents certain difficulties in that, to comprehend the source, we require to know something of the teaching itself, because it emanates from those planes of highly evolved consciousness which we are setting out to explore. Unless our ideas and our theories about Creation and the purpose of life on this planet are to be worked out on a kind of do-it-yourself basis, we must be prepared to recognise the existence of Beings who are of a quality quite different from ourselves. And this in turn requires the acceptance, as an act of faith for later confirmation or even rejection, of certain principles and hypotheses which are themselves a part of this esoteric knowledge pertaining to the Ageless Wisdom teaching.

In other words, we have at first to accept on faith that there is a teaching and a training made available to us by those who have attained to a far deeper spiritual awareness than even the most advanced intellectuals of our Age. And we have to accept this until such time as our own expanded sense of awareness converts our faith into belief, which is still only a product of the intelligence; and finally into the real conviction of the knower, as a result of a down-pouring of super-consciousness from the soul. I quote here an excerpt from the statement of The Tibetan which is given in full in the Appendix.

Introduction

If the writings present truth in such a way that it follows sequentially upon that already offered in the world teachings, if the information given raises the aspiration and the will-to-serve from the plane of the emotions to that of the mind (the plane whereon the Masters can be found) then they will have served their purpose. If the teaching conveyed calls forth a response from the illumed mind of the worker in the world, and brings a flashing forth of his intuition, then let that teaching be accepted. But not otherwise. If the statements meet with eventual corroboration, or are deemed true under the test of the Law of Correspondences, then that is well and good. But should this not be so, let not the student accept what is said.

What follows is not intended for the trained esotericist, but for those who seek a deeper meaning to life and know not quite where to begin. The world is moving into a new era due to changes in the quality of the energies that are streaming into our consciousness, which we will be examining in a later chapter. In this new phase of evolution there is an apparent increased desire for spiritual knowledge; youth is no longer prepared to accept the old shiboleths, and is challenging established authority all along the line. This may be in many ways unsettling, but it is an indication of increasing mental activity in the masses that demands recognition. In relation to spiritual matters, contem-

The Seed of Wisdom

plation of man's destiny is no longer confined to the mystic and the philosopher, but is fast becoming the concern of a far wider sector of humanity. Although the churches are less attended than they used to be, the demand for spiritual knowledge is today far greater, more sincere and widespread.

The purpose of this brief introduction to esotericism is to encourage others to find out for themselves whether, in the words of Dr. Raynor Johnson 'this particular pathway from the dense material world to the spiritual' may help them in their quest for a deeper sense of reality with which to broaden and supplement their religious affiliations, whatever these may be.

1
The Constitution of Man

To start at the beginning it is necessary to ask ourselves whether we really are convinced that there is a purpose, and therefore presumably a plan for the universe; this is not something that we can assume or gloss over without deep thought, for it is fundamental to our philosophy of life.

On the one hand we have the views which are typical of the atheistic attitude, and which are well expressed by Professor A. J. Ayer who tells us:

> I am not convinced by the arguments which seek to show that the universe as a whole is a teleological system; I think that there is no end to which it is directed, and a fortiori no end for which it has been designed. I do not believe that it was created or is governed by a supernatural intelligence.

At the other end of the scale we have ideas such as those expressed by Arthur W. Osborn in his book, The Expansion of Awareness. He says:

> It is my view that the whole phenomenal universe can be likened to a dream and our individual lives

The Seed of Wisdom

are a dream within the greater dream of the creative imagination of the Supreme.

So we are faced with the choice of purpose or chance. Either the universe is entirely attributable to the latter, which appears inconceivable, or else it is a planned creation of which even the so called laws of nature are a part.

Even the most confirmed materialist will recognise that matter, and even living beings, respond in a more or less predictable manner to these so called natural laws. It may be such an obvious and generally accepted law, as for example the Law of Gravity; or it may be the less well understood Law of Cause and Effect. But law there seems to be, and not chaos. The very existence of law and order implies reason behind it, and intelligence, and above all – purpose. It also implies a plan; and as there cannot be a plan without a planner, neither can we conceive of a creation without a Creator.

If we cannot accept this fundamental basis for an exploration into the meaning and purpose of our lives, then of course there is an end to the matter. The vast majority of thinking people would, however, be prepared to accept as an hypothesis, supported by reason and fortified by faith, that there is indeed a purpose and a plan for the universe and therefore the world in which we live our little lives; and that all creation and evolution is the result of the directed and

The Constitution of Man

continuing thought and energy of Will of a Higher intelligence that we call the Creator – or God.

Before any created thing is made manifest, it must first exist in the mind of its creator; and thus every act of creation is the result of thought. Thought is a factor of intelligence and, as we shall see later, energy follows thought. The process of creation is much the same whether that which is created is a garden, a building, a city; or a symphony or a painting; or a political organisation or a nation – or a universe. That which differs in every case is the factor of quality and of magnitude; quality of the creative mind and therefore of the thought-form, and again quality of the energy of will that drives the thought-form into manifestation. Where the energy of will or purposefulness is lacking the thought-form will fail to materialise, unless or until it may be picked up and materialised by someone else.

What – we may ask – is the source of these ideas, and therefore the forms? Is this always original, or is it not frequently the result of sub-conscious sensitivity to the thoughts of others? Do we have access to a common pool of ideas – accessible in lesser or greater measure in accordance with the quality of our mental equipment? As we ponder on these questions, do we sense the reality that the universe and all that exists within it is but the precipitation of thought-forms emanating continuously from the One Source?

Despite the statement that spiritual knowledge cannot be grasped by the use of the intellect alone, it is

The Seed of Wisdom

nevertheless necessary to obtain a basic intellectual understanding on which to build; and this is particularly true of our recognition of the esoteric world of energies and forces that distinguishes the teaching from the more usual concept of Creation as expounded in the orthodox Christian faith.

In addition to the hypothesis concerning the existence of a plan and a purpose for the universe, there are three further hypotheses which are fundamental to our theme, and these we will consider in the following chapters. They are:

1. There is nothing in the manifested universe that does not possess an energy form, subtle and intangible, yet substantial and which controls, governs and conditions the outer physical body. This is the etheric body.
2. Man is a soul and possesses a mortal body. It is not the other way round. Serving as a link between the soul and the dense physical body is an energy body vibrant with energies of life itself and of those energies and forces which condition its ever developing consciousness. This is the etheric body of man.
3. The soul, itself a vehicle of Spirit, through its vehicle which we term the etheric body, incarnates in dense physical form periodically and cyclicly until a degree of human perfection is attained that will release that soul so

The Constitution of Man

that it stands free in the realms of Higher Evolution.

It is surely obvious that it would be a gross understatement to say that there is much food for thought in these three fundamental hypotheses; and although the light of the intuition will in the end be essential for anything like full comprehension, a start can certainly be made by the use of the intellect.

Through this method he (the man) will grow, for the roots of intuitive knowledge are laid deep within the soul, and the soul therefore must be contacted before the intuition can work. The intuition reveals not the way ambition can be fed nor the manner in which desire for selfish advancement can be gratified.

For some readers this may be considered the right moment to begin the work of invoking, by meditation, the intuitive response. Others may have embarked already on this practice, whilst again others may long ago have acquired the art of deep meditation on spiritual matters without the urge for spiritual knowledge, which is the hall-mark of the mystic, as distinct from the occultist.

Comprehension of the Whole can never be achieved by a study of the part; and therefore what is required is quiet and deep meditation on the whole picture as slowly it comes into view. It is rather like cleaning an

The Seed of Wisdom

Old Master. We see the whole picture dimly and gradually the details appear as we clear away that which has kept them hidden. Without the whole vision, however dim, the details would be meaningless.

Gradually, through spiritual reading and meditation, a man acquires what Djwal Khul terms the esoteric sense, which he describes as follows:

> I mean essentially the power to live and function subjectively, to possess a constant inner contact with the soul and the world in which it is found, and this must work out subjectively through love, actively shown; through wisdom, steadily outpoured; and through that capacity to include and to identify oneself with all that breathes and feels, which is the outstanding characteristic of all truly functioning sons of God. I mean therefore, an interiorly held attitude of mind which can orient itself at will in any direction. It can govern and control the emotional sensitiveness, not only of the disciple himself, but of all he may contact. By the strength of his silent thought, he can bring light and peace to all. Through that mental power, he can tune in on the world of thought, and upon the realm of ideas and can discriminate between, and choose, those mental energies and those concepts which will enable him, as a worker under the plan, to influence his environment and to clothe the new ideals in thought matter which will enable them to be more easily

recognised in the world of ordinary thinking and living. This attitude of mind will enable the disciple also to orient himself to the world of souls, and to that high place of inspiration and of light, discover his fellow workers, communicate with them, and in unison with them collaborate in the working out of divine intentions.

This is high ambition in the best sense of the word; too high perhaps for most of us: but it is the attainment of this esoteric sense that, even in its earlier manifestation, can result in the ability to look instinctively for the underlying causes of events and of the problems that arise in our own lives and in the world around us. It is in fact, or at any rate it should be, our motive for seeking the knowledge, not as an end in itself, but for the purpose of its application to our daily living, so that it becomes wisdom bearing in mind that spiritual knowledge has been defined by D. K. as intelligent love.

2
The Etheric Body

MODERN SCIENTIFIC theory, developed mainly in the Western hemisphere, recognises that all matter is composed of atoms, which are themselves no more than positive and negative energies in action and reaction. We also know that these atoms are fused together (though this may not be a very scientific way of expressing it) into molecules, which are in turn moulded into myriads of forms held together by some mysterious energy or force that is vital to the forms. Just as the atom is dependent upon its positive centre around which the electrons move, so too is the solar system held together by the attractive energy of its central sun.

For thousands of years Eastern thought has predicated a vital energy underlying and interpenetrating all material forms; and in writing about this concept, Alice Bailey quotes from the writings of Ramacharaka as follows:

Prana, being the Sanscrit term meaning Absolute Energy, we may consider as the active principle of life – Vital Force, if you please. It is found in all

The Etheric Body

forms of life, from the amoeba to man, from the most elementary form of plant life to the highest form of animal life. It is found in all things having life, and as the occult philosophy teaches that life is in all things – in every atom – the apparent lifelessness of some things being only a lesser degree of manifestation, we may understand their teaching that Prana is everywhere in everything.

In the Eastern concept, the etheric or subtle body underlying all forms is the result of this vital force – Prana – acting on a universal element which is called Akasha, and which, in western thinking, we would term Ether. Arthur Osborn, in his book The Expansion of Awareness writes:

> A Psychic Ether is an attractive theory because it is near enough to our normal conceptions to make it thinkable . . . Provided we treat ether strictly as an hypothesis, it can aid our thinking about these difficult matters. But there is always the danger of the psychic ether becoming substantialised and regarded as having an independent existence.

So in building upon our hypothesis concerning the etheric body, we can certainly start by recognising that at the centre of every form is a focus of positive energy that we define as life; and this applies in every kingdom of nature from the mineral to the human kingdom and even, in a certain sense, beyond. With-

The Seed of Wisdom

draw this central vital force and the dense physical form will disintegrate together with the underlying etheric body, and its components, each with its tiny spark of vital force, are scattered; but the form in which they were incorporated has ceased to exist as such.

But man is more than this; for man is a soul manifesting, when in incarnation, through an etheric and a dense physical body. He is destined to register much more than just the energy of life, for it is the purpose of humanity to establish 'an outpost of the Christ consciousness (or Love/Wisdom aspect of the Creator) in the world of mental awareness'.

Thus in addition to his vital energy body, man is equipped with a mental-energy body which is the mind, and an emotional or desire body which we term the astral. It is the sum-total of these three which, when integrated and under the control of the mind, we term the personality – using the term in a somewhat different sense to the usual meaning of the word.

Through the etheric body streams the vital energy of life to the heart; to the head streams the *dual* energy of consciousness; desire or emotional energy through the astral body, and mental energy through the mental body.

This threefold energy body is that which, in the words of our first hypothesis, controls, governs and conditions the dense physical body. This is also the link between the soul and the dense physical body, which

The Etheric Body

was the substance of our second hypothesis. And it is the vehicle of the incarnating soul which is in turn the vehicle of Spirit, which is God in us.

Once again it is important at this stage to emphasise the difficulty – even the impossibility – of grasping this vast concept by the use of the intellect alone. But by meditation and pondering on the theme as a whole, and not by intellectual analysis and demand for proof of every statement, understanding will come and a dawning of the esoteric sense.

The whole concept of creative purpose working through streams of divine energy directed to the forms in all the kingdoms of nature from the human down to the dense mineral, using the etheric body as a link between the soul and its dense physical expression, needs constantly to be borne in mind.

But the etheric body of man is, as one would expect, an immensely more complicated mechanism than that of the less evolved sub-human kingdoms. It is the degree of consciousness that is the determining factor.

The etheric body is composed of interlocking and circulating lines of force, emanating from one or other, or from one or many, of the seven planes or areas of consciousness of our planetary life. It has seven major centres, which respond to the inflowing energies of the greater life.

The dense physical body, composed of atoms, each with its own individual life, light and activity,

The Seed of Wisdom

is held together and is expressive of the energies which compose the etheric body.

As a man's attitude, attainment and comprehension shift to ever higher levels, the etheric body will be constantly changing and responding to the newer energies the man will purposely attract.'

This etheric body permeates every part of the dense physical form and extends some few inches beyond the perimeter of the latter. As an energy body it is also a body of light and can be seen by the clairvoyant in colours which vary in accord with the emotional and mental moods and condition of the person. Until quite recently, such a statement would have been greeted with derision by scientists; but the medical profession is very slowly becoming aware of the subtle energies that influence the physical state of the body. Highly qualified neuro-psychiatrists are researching into this field, and more will be said of these researches when we come to the subject of the seven major centres of energy in the etheric body.

The mental and the emotional energy bodies can be visualised in very much the same way, for they too are bodies of light that change in relation to the man's spiritual development. This is probably the origin of the halo depicted in religious paintings of the Christ and the Saints as descriptive of the radiance of the head centre when in full activity.

The etheric body, which has been called the outer

The Etheric Body

garment of the soul, 'outlives' the dense physical form for a short while, as indeed it preceded the birth of the physical body as we know it. The death of the physical body can be thought of as mechanical failure due to the normal process of wear and tear or to accident, and what we might call a second death takes place when the etheric body is dissipated and the focus of consciousness is withdrawn to what is termed the Kama-manasic body in the case of an integrated personality whose emotional or desire body is largely under the control of the mental. Where this is not the case, the focus of consciousness, on the death of the physical and etheric sheaths, becomes centred in the astral or desire body. This subject will be enlarged upon in a later chapter on the subject of reincarnation. Suffice it to say at this point that, when in exceptional cases this withdrawal of consciousness to deeper levels of being is arrested for some reason, such as acute distress and unwillingness to abandon the physical world, the etheric body may linger-on for a while. This might perhaps be a possible explanation of hauntings.

The focus of consciousness in the astral body immediately after death may also be a possible explanation of cases which are known, and supported by reliable evidence, of people killed in accidents or in the war making their presence felt, at the time of their death, to others who at the time were thousands of miles away in another country. It could well be that the astral body, freed from the restrictions of the dense physical, may be more 'mobile' on the inner levels of consciousness – conjectural, but worth considering.

But to return to the subject of the etheric body:
The etheric body is primarily composed of the dominant energy or energies to which the man, the group, the nation or the world reacts in any particular life cycle or world period . . . and the extent to which the energies can become a dominant feature of the man's life is dependent upon the development and the functioning of the seven major centres in the etheric body.

The source of these energies, whether divine or otherwise, and whether they come to us via the soul, or from other human beings via the emotional body, will be discussed later but first we should have a clear understanding of the mechanism by means of which these energies are registered in the etheric body and communicated to the dense physical.

3
Energy Centres and the Endocrine Glands

ON THE one hand, the science of the etheric centres has been handed down for thousands of years through the holy men of the East by word of mouth to their disciples, as well as in their scriptures. On the other hand, endocrinology – the medical science of the endocrine glands – is a comparatively new branch of medical knowledge in the light of which the ancient science of the etheric body and its energy centres would probably be relegated to the realms of science fiction. Nevertheless, when we consider these two branches of knowledge as complimentary to each other, the result is impressive.

Our hypothesis is that man's physical, emotional, mental and spiritual condition, as well as his potential, are dependent upon firstly, the state of development of the seven major energy centres in the etheric body; and secondly the manner in which the incoming energies are communicated by the centres to their counterparts in the physical body which, as we shall see, are the endocrine glands or, as they are also termed, the ductless glands.

Energies of many types – spiritual, mental,

The Seed of Wisdom

emotional and vital – emanating from many sources – extra-planetary, planetary, from our environment, our community, our family and friends stream into the etheric body through the seven energy centres. The extent to which the energies are properly registered in a beneficial and harmonious manner is dependent upon the activity of the centres and this is an all important factor in human evolution.

To the extent that the centres are active in a man, the incoming energies will be registered and will be communicated to the endocrine gland which is located in close juxtaposition to each of the seven centres. To the extent that the glands are functioning correctly the energies will be distributed to the physical body via the blood stream and the nervous system.

As we shall see, average man functions in response to no more than the activity of those centres which are intended to register the basic energies essential to the life of the physical body and to the sentient, astral or emotional aspects of living. Mental energy, and what we might term spiritual energy are not fully registered until the corresponding higher centres have become active as a result of the evolutionary drive which, over the ages and the many incarnations enables the soul to acquire an etheric body adequate for the purpose.

The location of the seven energy centres in the etheric body are:

1. The head centre. *pineal*
2. The centre between the eyebrows. *pituitary*

Energy Centres and the Endocrine Glands

3. The throat centre. *thyroid gland*
4. The heart centre. — *thymus*
5. The solar plexus centre. *pancreas*
6. The centre at the base of the spine. *adrenals*
7. The sacral centre. *gonads*

The head centre, situated in the etheric body, outside but directly over the top of the head, is said to be active only in the most spiritually advanced types of human beings. It registers the energy of spiritual will, or purpose, and is dynamic in quality. It has been described as the seat of the soul, and is said to remain active during infancy until the will-to-be is sufficiently established so that the soul is firmly anchored in physical incarnation. Otherwise it is relatively inactive until the man has acquired a heightened degree of spiritual consciousness; until he has experienced a certain expansion of awareness and can be said to be a soul-infused personality, and therefore one to be entrusted with the energy of will and spiritual power.

The head centre in the etheric body has its counterpart in the endocrine system of the dense physical body. This is the pineal gland imbedded in the brain at the top of the head. Significantly, very little is known about the physical function of this ductless gland, neither has its hormone been identified. We do know that it is stimulated by the use of certain drugs such as L. S. D. and this may possibly account for the sense of enhanced spiritual awareness that is said to be

The Seed of Wisdom

induced by the use of these drugs. But their use is unlikely to result in anything other than harm if the physical gland is stimulated artificially, instead of naturally through the eventual activity of the head centre.

The centre between the eyebrows, usually known as the ajna centre, can be the most powerful energy centre active in all those human beings who have progressed above the stage of automatic, unthinking and instinctual living; and who are integrated personalities functioning at the mental level. The activity of this centre produces idealism and gives impulse to the truly creative function. The caste mark to be seen in the centre of the forehead of high-caste Hindus is symbolic of this stage of spiritual development. Its physical counterpart in the endocrine system is the pituitary, located at the base of the brain cavity and therefore in close proximity to the etheric centre between the eyebrows.

Endocrinologists consider the pituitary gland to be the most important centre for the production of hormones, including amongst others the hormone A C T H now widely used in medicine to reduce inflamation. The pituitary is also recognised as having a harmonising influence on the other ductless glands; and this physical attribute coincides perfectly with the activity of the ajna centre as it takes over energy control from the lower centres in the man who has hitherto functioned entirely at the emotional – desire level.

The throat centre is situated in the etheric body at the top of the spinal column outside the back of the neck. It is the first of the higher centres to become active when the man is beginning to develop spiritual awareness; and it is the centre through which the intelligence aspect of humanity is energised, particularly when demonstrating creative ability. Its physical agency in the endocrine system is the thyroid gland, close to the larynx and concerned with brain activity, intellectual development, perceptivity and all that is of most importance in the transitional period from instinct to intellect.

The heart centre, in the etheric equivalent of the spine, at about the level of the shoulder blades, is the receiver and distributor of the energy of love-wisdom. Until this centre becomes active, the energy of love may be said to by-pass the inactive centre and become focussed in the solar plexus centre where it registers as the emotion of desire. Later, when the man has brought his desire nature under the control of the mind, and the man is turning attention to spiritual things and becoming group conscious, desire is transmuted into love through the activity of the heart centre. D. K. tells us:

Upon the unfoldment of the heart centre, and on an

The Seed of Wisdom

intelligent relation of mankind to the Hierarchy, with the consequent response of man to the energy of love, all disciples are asked at this time to ponder and reflect, for 'as a man thinketh in his heart, so is he'. Thinking in the heart becomes truly possible only when the mental faculties have been adequately developed and have reached a fairly high state of unfoldment. Feeling in the heart is often confused with thinking. The ability to think in the heart is the result of the process of transmuting desire into love during the task of elevating the forces of the solar plexus into the heart centre . . . Thinking as a result of correct feeling is then substituted for personal sensitivity.

In the physical body, the corresponding endocrine gland is the thymus, located in the upper part of the chest. Strangely enough, relatively little is known about this gland, although it is said to be closely connected with the activity and control of the vagus nerve and nervous system.

These four centres of the etheric body, situated above the diaphragm, are those which are in full activity, or are becoming so, only in the man who is an integrated personality, whose sentient nature is at the command of the mind, and whose whole state of awareness is an open channel for the energy of love-wisdom and soul expression in that man's life. This does not mean to say that these centres above the dia-

Energy Centres and the Endocrine Glands

phragm are entirely quiescent in the many thousands of aspirants throughout the world, who are gradually bringing the etheric body, and therefore the physical form, under the control of mental energy and who are thus responding to the divine plan for humanity.

Unevolved or savage man responds simply to vital energy and the appetites of the lower nature. Average man is impulsed mainly by desire; and these two groups, which embrace millions of ordinary, sensitive and kindly people are activated almost exclusively by the energies flowing through the two powerful centres below the diaphragm – The solar plexus centre and the sacral centre.

The first of these, the solar plexus centre, is located in the etheric counterpart of the spine, approximately in the middle section behind the stomach. This is the instinctual centre and the seat of the emotions. We are told that it is the centre in the etheric body through which the mass of average and unenlightened humanity lives and moves and has its being. The solar plexus in the physical body is the largest sympathetic nerve centre in animal-man and is the centre of instinctual functioning. It is activated by the ductless glands in the endocrine system known as the pancreas, which produce insulin, vital to the metabolism of sugar, and therefore muscular power, and also of importance to the digestive system.

The second of these etheric centres below the diaphragm is the sacral centre, situated behind the

The Seed of Wisdom

lumbar region of the spine, and the physical correspondences are the male and female sex glands. This was the first of the etheric centres to attain full functioning activity in the human race millions of years ago in the Lemurian Age.

The third of the etheric centres below the diaphragm, and the last of the seven centres we are here dealing with so briefly, is known as the centre at the base of the spine, simply because that is where it is located. Although its physical correspondence in the endocrine system are the adrenal glands, producing adrenalin, so essential to immediate active response to danger, the etheric centre is relatively quiescent and only aroused to full activity by an act of will on the part of the most highly evolved man himself. The importance of this centre will become apparent when, in a later chapter, we consider the types of force that are pouring through these centres and the evolutionary effect in the body of humanity as the incoming energies can increasingly be handled by the etheric centres above the diaphragm.

The main objective of this chapter is to establish in the mind of the reader the mechanism through which the dense physical body of man responds to the energies flowing through the etheric centres in the subtle bodies – mental, emotional and vital; and the relationship between these energy centres and their physical counterparts. These can be summarised, for ready reference, as follows:

Energy Centres and the Endocrine Glands

Etheric Centres	Endocrine Glands
Head centre	Pineal
Ajna centre	Pituitary
Throat centre	Thyroid
Heart centre	Thymus
Solar plexus centre	Pancreas
Sacral centre	Gonads
Base of the spine	Adrenals

The activity of the centres, and the interdependence of the endocrine glands, are well illustrated by two quotations from widely differing sources relating to the same fundamental truth.

The first of these is from the Tibetan, in Alice Bailey's book, Esoteric Healing:

> The danger involved in a large number of physical ills can be traced to the condition of the centres, to their interplay or their lack of interplay, to an undeveloped condition, unawakened and sluggish, and to an overstimulation or an unbalanced activity. If one centre is prematurely awakened, it is frequently at the expense of other centres.

The second is from a strictly scientific source in a statement by Dr. Peter Stephan, an endocrinologist who is the Principal of the Cell Therapy Centre in London, he writes:

> Hidden away in various parts of the body, the endocrine glands all have partners, each compli-

mentary to the other and all interdependent, which means that if one is out of order then, sooner or later, the rest are affected ... Many organic disorders are merely the result of glandular dysfunction.

Yes indeed, and we might add – glandular dysfunction as a result of the misuse of energy, or resulting from the temporary upset in the balance of the energy centres as the man shifts his focus of living from the purely physical to the emotional and then to mental levels.

It may be appropriate to end this chapter with a further quotation from Esoteric Healing written twenty years ago:

> I have indicated the areas conditioned by the centres, and far more powerfully conditioned than you have any means yet of ascertaining; I have said that fundamentally the ductless glands (endocrine glands), as externalisations of the centres, are the determining factors in the health of the body; and that where there is imbalance, over-development or under-development, you will have trouble: I have suggested that the medical profession in the New Age will deal increasingly with the theory of energy direction and its relation to the ductless glands, and that it will admit, at least hypothetically and for the purpose of experimentation, that the theory of the energy centres may be correct and that they are the primary conditioning factors, working through the

Energy Centres and the Endocrine Glands

ductless glands which, in their turn, guard the body, produce the necessary resistance, keep the blood stream supplied with the essentials to health and – when rightly related – produce a balanced expression of the spiritual man throughout the entire physical body – physiological and psychological balance. When this desirable condition is not the case, then the ductless glands, through wrong relationship and incorrect and unbalanced development, are not adequate to the task; they cannot protect the body from disease, and are unable to pour into the bloodstream what the physical vehicle needs. Owing to their inadequacy, the body is unable to resist infections, is in a constant state of ill-health and cannot cope with disease coming from without or latent within the organism of the body; this weakness often produces mortal disease.

What needs to be emphasised is that physical man can only respond adequately to spiritual energy to the extent that this mechanism of the etheric centres is in active and balanced operation. This is only achieved once a human being is past the stage of animal-man; a stage that is attained through conscious co-operation between the physical vehicle, the personality and the indwelling soul as a result of mental activity or mystical experience induced by deep thought and meditation, or through intense spiritual devotion, or both.

4
The Soul and the Doctrine of Re-birth

IN THE preceding chapters we have considered, in outline, certain hypotheses concerning the etheric body of all created things and then, in particular, the etheric body of man with its seven centres for the reception of those energies which distinguish man from all other living creatures. We have, in other words been studying the vehicle of the human soul when incarnate, in an attempt to understand the divine plan and the role of humanity in that plan.

Before we can proceed very much further, we have to face up to the extremely difficult question of just what exactly is the human soul. And although at first sight it may appear to be an evasion of the question, the most helpful statement is that just as the threefold personality – comprising the mental, emotional and etheric bodies – is the vehicle of the soul, so the soul is the vehicle of Spirit. But why, we may ask, is this intermediate vehicle between Spirit and the personality necessary? Why cannot Spirit manifest directly through the personality?

Perhaps the best answer is that, in the end, the Spirit does so manifest; but only after a personality has been developed whose mechanism is sufficiently perfected to register and to manifest the divine quality; so that, as a result, man is made perfect in the image of God. But why cannot God, with his infinite power of creation, bring this perfection to pass at a stroke? Why does He tolerate the imperfection that gives rise to so much misery in His world? Surely the answer to this oft-repeated question is that the perfect image must include, as part of its perfection, the quality of free will. Man is not to be just an automaton of his Creator, but is to include in his final perfection this quality of ruling his own destiny.

But the process, and the path to perfection is an exceedingly long one, and no ordinary vehicle of manifestation has yet emerged that can stand up to more than about a hundred years of usage; and this is because man has yet to learn how to register the creative energies so that they are not diverted and distorted by man's own selfishness and wrong thinking. For it is this that destroys the human body through disease and wasting.

If the threefold personality and its dense physical counterpart is unable to persist for the aeons required to achieve perfection, then what is to be the vehicle that can carry over from one short life to another the small advance that is normally achieved in a single lifetime? The answer is – the soul.

The soul is the storehouse of the experiences of worthwhile value gained by the man in each successive incarnation. On the dispersion of the etheric body following the death of the physical, the soul withdraws; in fact the withdrawal is often the cause rather than the result of death. On withdrawal the soul retains in consciousness a memory or record of the state of activity of the etheric centres, for the purpose of beginning the next reincarnation with equipment at least as responsive as that which was relinquished at the close of the previous incarnation. The same process is repeated by the soul, life after life, with respect to all three energy components of the personality – etheric, astral and mental; and this is in fact the mechanism of rebirth.

The soul has an existence or consciousness of its own, whether in physical incarnation or not: and that soul is the real man – the self as distinct from the not-self. The physical body, and also that which we have termed the personality, have *their* areas of consciousness, which are other than that of the soul. What needs to be emphasised is that during his life on earth man eventually attains a dual consciousness; that of the soul and that of his vehicle of manifestation.

In primitive man, and even in the lower ranges of average man, his vehicle of incarnation, and in particular that aspect of it which we term the lower mind or mental body, is almost totally unaware of the soul, and therefore at this stage there is no conflict. Animal comforts and desires, love and affection, are all he desires, except perhaps the sub-conscious urge to

The Soul and the Doctrine of Re-birth

evolve. But as he evolves, the lower mind and the brain become more sensitive to the in-pouring energies as the centres become more active. The first link in consciousness is between the mental body and the mental aspect of the soul. Up to this point the soul has taken little account of his successive vehicles of incarnation, knowing that there could be no response from them until the centres had developed sufficient activity to register soul energy in the consciousness of the man.

Once this response is registered, the conflict begins between the self-willed personality and the indwelling soul, and this is the experience that we are conscious of as we live out our daily lives. Perhaps we recognise this in its early stages as the 'still small voice' of the conscience; but later we begin to sense the reality of the soul within, and later still, much later, comes the recognition of our one-ness or, we might say, our at-one-ment with the Whole. It is the achievement of this recognition that is – or should be – the objective of all religious thought and aspiration. 'Recognition by the part of its relation to the Whole, plus a constantly growing awareness of that relation'.

Finally, D.K. tells us:

> when the power of the soul is being imposed upon the personality, then the energy of the soul supersedes the other energies and the personality – focussed in the mind and responsive to soul impression – expresses on the physical plane

The Seed of Wisdom

(through the medium of the physical brain and body) the intent, potency and nature of the all inclusive soul.

And so we return to that perplexing question; what *is* the soul? Here are some statements which may or may not help us in our search for a definition:

> The embodied life of God, coming into incarnation to reveal the quality of the nature of God, which is essential love.
> The One Life manifesting through matter produces a third factor which is consciousness. This is the Soul of all things.
> It is the quality which every form manifests.
> It is aliveness, awareness and consciousness.

The truth is that it is an unknown quantity that defies definition, and which is dependent for description on our own particular state of spiritual awareness. To some it is accepted as an act of blind faith; to others it is a reality concerning which there is no possible doubt.

It is a reality to those who know the Soul to be a fact in their own experience, but are unable to prove it, nor express satisfactorily to the man who admits only that which the concrete mind can grasp.

For me, at present, it is a re-incarnating unit of divine consciousness – which is the 'I' of each of us; and to re-capitulate briefly what has been said so far

The Soul and the Doctrine of Re-birth

concerning the Soul and the doctrine of re-birth, it could be expressed as follows.

The soul lives, or let us say, is conscious perpetually in or on its own plane of consciousness which is the 5th Kingdom of nature – the Kingdom of God of the Christian Bible. The soul periodically 'clothes' itself – or rather a fraction of itself – with a threefold energy body composed of mental, astral and etheric energies, for the purpose of incarnation in the dense physical world. But even during these periods the habitat of the soul is on its own plane of consciousness.

Incarnation for the soul is a period of experiment, experience and expression.

At the end of each incarnation the soul withdraws its incarnating spark back into the consciousness of the whole, with a recognition of the accomplishments and failures of the experience, and a knowledge of what needs to be done next time.

Little by little, life after life, the soul learns through experience to recognise its purpose, to understand the qualifying energies and to communicate them to his vehicles of expression in the field of manifestation. He learns to express in the world of experience all that is concerned with understanding and relationship. He can then express *active* harmlessness, which is not negative; compassion, that is not just pity; love, that is not just emotional and wisdom, which is intelligent love. He recognises the purpose of the Plan, and the

The Seed of Wisdom

direction that his service to the Plan shall take.

Very many spiritually orientated people, who accept the well established belief in the immortality of the soul, find it difficult – and many find it distasteful – to accept the doctrine of re-incarnation. A few are confused by the rubbish that is sometimes referred to as the transmigration of souls, which is supposed to include the possibility of human souls being reborn in animal forms of the third kingdom of nature. This misconception is merely the result of misunderstanding of an ancient doctrine distorted by ignorance and superstition. By the term reincarnation or re-birth we mean the re-birth of the human soul in human form. Others find difficulty in understanding why, if the doctrine is true, we cannot remember our past lives. It is of course perfectly true that we have no such memory but, as Arthur Osborn points out in his book The Expansion of Awareness: if it requires the skilled techniques of psycho-analysis to recall from the subconscious mind certain memories of even our present lives, just imagine the techniques that would be required to recall the memory of our past lives. He says:

> I am rather disposed to think that after death our present life will become subconscious, relative to our after-death waking consciousness.

So, although most of us have experienced that vague sensation of 'having been here before', it is only those

The Soul and the Doctrine of Re-birth

very few who are reported to remember a previous incarnation, who can count on such recollection as evidence – for them at least – of pre-existence. Here again I quote from Arthur Osborn:

> However, even thousands of such cases would not, I think, constitute proof of reincarnation, but they might provide strong presumptions in its favour, and perhaps even an intuitive conviction that it was true. This of course would be more likely to occur if one were satisfied on general principles that re-incarnation is a reasonable theory.

The best way of making up our own minds as to whether any theory is reasonable or not, is to satisfy ourselves first of all that the source of the doctrine emanates from a serious and properly authenticated school of thought, and then to accept it as an hypothesis to be tested in the light of experience and the application of intellectual and intuitive reason.

In relation to the doctrine of re-incarnation the realisation that this life on earth is but a short and fleeting moment in the long life of the soul goes a long way to explain the apparent injustice of the misery we see in the lives of millions who have done nothing in this particular life to account for their unhappy state. This life may be only a passing phase of intense suffering, in which some lesson, such as fortitude, or compassion, or humility may have to be learnt to

The Seed of Wisdom

compensate, under the law of cause and effect, for the 'karma' built up in earlier lives.

Reincarnation could explain the wisdom so often found in an uneducated peasant; the occasional brilliance and genius of the child prodigy; and above all the example of the very few who live a life of near perfection. It is perhaps that these have, as souls, lived longer and learnt faster.

If, as Christians, we accept the doctrine of the immortality of the soul, is it not reasonable to suppose that if the soul is indeed immortal it must have a consciousness of its own that is not dependent upon the body? Why, then, should not this consciousness of the soul be a reality not only after, but also prior to, earthly existence? We can of course take the view that each human soul incarnates for a single lifetime on earth and then returns whence it came. At least this theory would have the merit of focussing the quality of consciousness in the soul rather than the mortal body; but somehow it still lacks conviction, even if only because so little is ever achieved in the course of a single lifetime that, except in relatively few cases, the experience of incarnation seems so incomplete.

The Christian teaching is not alone in its contention that the basic sin, which embraces all others, consists in the hurt we cause to our fellow beings or to our community or environment; but who, other than He Who showed us the way, has ever managed to lead an actively harmless life in the short span of a single

The Soul and the Doctrine of Re-birth

lifetime? The teaching anent rebirth holds out the same hope to saint and sinner alike, but instead of condemning the sinner to a state of eternal damnation, proclaims the truth of redemption and re-dress rather than forgiveness. Under the hypothesis of rebirth the soul is the indwelling entity that is seeking to *manifest* perfection and is, as it were, drawn back into incarnation to redress the failures of past lives; to compensate for harm done and to continue on the long path to perfection.

Finally the lessons are learnt, the centres are vibrant with energy, and then, in one triumphant life the soul demonstrates – for this is the purpose – demonstrates in physical incarnation the qualities of love, wisdom, compassion and selflessness. Then can that soul be free from the illusions of the astral/physical life; free too from the trials and tribulations of life on earth, unless for the supreme experience, as an act of free will, of returning to show the way so that others may follow, before that Soul enters on the path of the Higher Evolution. And this was the substance of the third of the three hypotheses which we formulated in the first chapter of this book.

Eventually the truth is recognised that even the soul is mortal, though on quite a different time scale. We then know the truth that now we can only sense; that the soul is the vehicle of Spirit just as the personality was the vehicle of the soul. At this stage it would seem that we have, in a sense, linked up once more with the

The Seed of Wisdom

Christian doctrine in that, at the end of the long life of the soul, there seems to be an existence very akin to the Christian concept of Heaven, concerning which we can know nothing.

Somehow this seems to make so much more sense to the intuition, and seems to be so much more in accordance with what Christ was trying to tell us, than the Church doctrine that having spent, with relatively few exceptions, a pretty selfish and often wasted life of three score years and ten, we are entitled to pass on to the glory of heaven – unless we are despatched elsewhere for having gone a bit too far in our transgressions.

These are some of the criteria we can ponder; and consider whether our hypothesis concerning the doctrine of reincarnation is reasonable. As for an 'intuitive conviction' we can only study and meditate until the light breaks through.

5
On Evolution

ALL FORMS, in all the kingdoms of nature, are but the vehicles of creative energy; and at every level of creation evolution is taking place – evolution towards a more expressive state of being. In the first, or mineral, kingdom we find life, even though, as Ramacharaka has said, the apparent lifelessness of some things is merely a lesser degree of manifestation. Vital energy is in action in the mineral kingdom, though not emotional or mental energy as in the higher kingdoms of nature. Nevertheless, when we consider the radio-active minerals with their dynamic potential, and the beauty of the precious stones and metals, can we not sense that even here evolution is at work.

In the second, or vegetable, kingdom we find, in addition to the basic energy of life, the demonstration of sensitivity to a far higher degree than in the mineral kingdom. Served by the lower kingdom which provides its requirements for physical life, it in turn serves the animal and human kingdoms; whilst evolution is to be seen on every hand in the form of colour, scent, beauty and service.

The Seed of Wisdom

In the animal kingdom we find, not only greatly increased sentient and emotional energy, but also the manifestation of mental energy as evolution, aided by man, proceeds. The qualities of affection, faithfulness and intelligence are developed; and once again we should note the dependence on the lower kingdom and the up-looking towards the higher. Not only is the process of evolution plain for all to see, but what is worth while noting is the effort of the domesticated animals to understand what is required of them by the fourth kingdom of man, for them their gods.

Primitive animal-man millions of years ago in the Lemurian Age was concerned with the development of his vital physical form. He was, so to speak learning to function mechanically. Later, in the Atlantean Age, hundreds of thousands of years ago, he was concerned with the development of his astral or emotional body, with very little mental capacity except in the case of the fore-runners of the race. Still later, at the commencement of our present Aryan Age, the focus of man's consciousness was beginning to shift to the mental level. This may well be the explanation of the legend of Adam and Eve – the beginning of knowledge.

The history of man's evolution can be seen in the development of every child from birth. Maurice Bucke, in his book Cosmic Consciousness, points out that the new-born child acquires his senses and develops them in exactly the same order as mankind

On Evolution

as a race has done. He then suggests that the stability of any particular sense in modern man is a factor of time. Thus whilst the earlier evolved senses such as touch and taste are completely stable, hearing and sight are not so stable, hence the phenomena of colour blindness and the birth of the deaf and dumb. Hence also the frequency of complete lack of any moral sense, which was developed in man at a far later stage in his evolution.

There is no reason to suppose that man has exhausted all the possibilities of developing his senses; and today we find serious and valuable research into extra-sensory perception in the field of consciousness, as distinct from lower forms of E.S.P., such as clairvoyance and clairaudience, which are a relic of the past.

The evolution of the animal form, and in particular the development of the underlying energy body and the receptivity of the centres resulted, millions of years ago, in the advent of humanity, when man became the vehicle of what we might call a soul of his own; the animals being ensouled in groups. This is crudely expressed, partly because of the inadequacy of our language for the purpose of expressing these deeply esoteric teachings; and partly because our understanding of these great mysteries is so very limited by our individual state of spiritual awareness.

It is perhaps a new thought to some that the soul is

The Seed of Wisdom

organising itself for effort, re-orientating its forces, and preparing for a fresh and powerful impulse, but so it is. All forms of life under the force of evolution pass from initiation to initiation and the soul is not exempt from the process. Just as the soul of animal-man became united with another divine principle, and so brought into being the fourth kingdom in nature, so the soul in humanity is seeking contact with another divine aspect. When that contact is made the Kingdom of God will come on earth; the physical plane will thereby be transformed and that peculiar period, presented symbolically under the term millenium, will come.

What needs emphasising is that, whilst evolution within each kingdom is all the time taking place, at the upper end is the aspiration to break through to the higher kingdom. This is however a soul aspiration, for it is the purpose of the human soul fully to express in physical form the potential of the divine qualities. When this is accomplished the new kingdom of what we might call soul-manifesting-humanity will appear.

Any hypothesis concerning the spiritual evolution of man should, I believe, take into account three separate but interdependent aspects of evolution, relating to the dense physical body, the etheric body and the soul.

Concerning the dense physical we need to be practical and realistic with regard to genetics and the

On Evolution

doctrine of the survival of the fittest. Physical forms survive in the long run only to the extent that they can adjust themselves to the changing conditions of life on the planet. Whilst this results from natural selection and adaptation, the intelligence and ingenuity of man also play an important part. By his brilliance in the field of medicine and surgery together with the newer sciences of radiology, psychology, psychiatry, endocrinology, and many others too numerous to mention, man has succeeded in extending the life of the dense physical body. Through his ambition and competitive nature, and his knowledge of genetics, the physical forms in all the kingdoms of nature are being refined and improved by breeding.

> It is the purpose of humanity to produce the forms of the required calibre to express the evolving quality of the indwelling soul at every level of human development.

With regard to the second component of our hypothesis, we are concerned with the conscious or unconscious development of the etheric centres, which we discussed in chapter 3. In the early stages of incarnation man is hardly conscious, if conscious at all, of this aspect of his evolution, but once the three subtle bodies – mental, emotional and etheric or vital – have been integrated into an embryo personality, sensitivity to the evolutionary energies can be greatly increased

The Seed of Wisdom

as a result of conscious effort through meditation and the application of knowledge.

These first two aspects of human evolution are succinctly expressed in the following statement by the Tibetan when outlining the process by which a human soul becomes incarnate. He asks us to regard as foundational and factual that the soul has:

(a) Appropriated a physical body of a certain calibre, adequate to the requirements and age of that soul.
(b) Energised that physical body through the medium of the etheric body, thus galvanising it into life activity for the duration of the Soul's set term of physical enterprise.

The third aspect of the evolution of man concerns the progress that the soul itself makes, not only whilst incarnate on earth, but also between incarnations. It would certainly not appear reasonable to suppose that all spiritual progress is halted during periods when the soul is not experiencing physical manifestation. Indeed, we are told that when the less evolved type of man is living a life of total envelopment in the little personal self on earth, almost unaware of his real self, the soul can do no more than attend to its affairs in the higher kingdom; knowing that later the experience of incarnation will be more fruitful.

Each one of us must work out his own philosophy of life, in accordance with the principle of free-will; but

On Evolution

it appears to me that the most essential feature of any such philosophy must be flexibility, by which I mean adaptability to the changes that must take place in our thinking as our sense of spiritual awareness expands and the light of the intuition breaks through. As I see it at present, the hypothesis I would like to work on is that the evolution of the whole man is a threefold process embracing that of the dense physical with emphasis on the brain, that of the personality with emphasis on the etheric body and its seven centres of energy, and that of the soul on its own plane.

We have been told that all beings pass through the experience of incarnation in human form, and do so repeatedly and cyclically until they achieve the full expression of Love, Wisdom and Intelligence. When this perfection is attained, then all desire for the separated self vanishes, and all desire for material things ceases. The Karma of past lives has been compensated and the man stands free; free to enter on the Path of the Higher Evolution where the Hierarchy of Masters is to be found, in which the Christ is the Highest Figure of Perfection.

Christ came to end the cycle of the emotional approach (to religion) which had existed since Atlantean days: He demonstrated in Himself the visioned perfection and then presented to humanity an example – in full manifestation – of every possibility latent in man *up to that time*. The achieving

The Seed of Wisdom

of the perfection of the Christ – Conciousness became the emphasised goal of humanity; the activity of all previous teachers and demonstrating Sons of God became only the presentation of the various aspects of a divine perfection which the Christ summarised in Himself. But he did far more than just this. Had this been all that He accomplished, He would have presented to humanity a picture of a static achievement, a culmination of perfection such as the evolutionary status of man at that time demanded; He would have given us, in fact, a Figure of very great, but at the same time, arrested development. This was of course impossible, but the religion which he founded has never recognised this fact or considered what lay beyond Christ, what was the nature of *His* subjective background and what was His point of achievement and whether He still had other possibilities. This was perhaps an unavoidable omission, owing to the fact that the idea of evolution was unknown until relatively very late in the human consciousness. Orthodox religion has been preoccupied with an emotional and aspirational approach to this Figure of Perfection; it has not looked beyond the Figure to the Reality which He represents.   This Christ Himself foresaw as a possibility and sought to obviate when He pointed out to His disciples that they could do 'greater things' than He had done because He was going 'to the Father'. He, in those

On Evolution

words, pointed beyond Himself to the ONE WHO was responsible for His Being and to the Way of the Higher Evolution – a subject with which the Church has never satisfactorily dealt. In the above words He indicated a state of being which He had never demonstrated on earth, owing to the unpreparedness of man and also to the fact that He Himself was only 'on His Way'.

This quotation should provoke thought on the distinction between the incarnating Spirit, in this case the Christ, and His manifestation in human form, on this occasion Jesus of Nazareth. We can sense the purpose of human evolution to manifest the evolving quality of the Soul at every level of human development. Perhaps it clarifies too what was earlier said with reference to Beings of a quality quite other than our own, though Human Beings nevertheless, from Whom the teaching reaches us through the media of the orthodox religions, the saints and mystics who, in the short span of a few thousand years have made contact, through prayer, meditation and contemplation, with what we might term the outposts of the Spiritual Hierarchy. In more recent times the channel has been widened by the more mental approach of the esotericists, philosophers and intellectuals who think-through the knowledge and help to bring it within the reach of those who have the will to invoke the response from higher mental levels.

6
The World of Energies

It was suggested earlier in this book to work on the hypothesis that all visible forms are an expression of underlying energy bodies which are the medium through which the creative and evolutionary energies – and other forces – are communicated to the man as an individual and to humanity as a whole.

At every level of consciousness – instinctual, emotional, mental and intuitional or spiritual – people are sensitive to other people, groups are sensitive to other groups and to individuals within the group and to others outside their particular sector of the community. Hence the power of leadership, the antagonism of political parties, the influence of public opinion, and the phenomenon of mass hysteria. Normally we tend to think of these influences as emanating from the individuals or groups themselves as we see them, without considering the enormously complicated pattern of underlying energies which are the cause of our reactions; nor do we stop to consider the powerful forces that emanate from our environment as a result of past history.

The planet is an organism in which the relationship

The World of Energies

between the kingdoms of nature and the planet itself is similar to the relationship between the organs of a human being and his whole body; whilst the individual units of life on the planet can be likened to the cells of the human body. The microcosm is a reflection of the macrocosm, and can be seen to be so when we consider the construction of the atom and that of the solar system or the universe and just as the component parts of the planet are 'ensouled', either individually as in the case of man, or in groups as in the lower kingdoms of nature, so also is a Nation or a political party 'ensouled' in the sense that it is the vehicle for certain energies and forces that are expressing themselves through form; and the planet itself is no exception.

Without wishing to complicate the picture unnecessarily, it should I think be mentioned here that the Earth, and indeed all the heavenly bodies are embodiments of great Spiritual Beings, Whose origins we are told lie outside the solar system altogether. It is an astounding concept to assimilate but, were this not the case, the homogeneous structure and the perfection of creative purpose would be impaired.

To return to our immediate subject of the energies and forces which condition humanity and the individual, we shall see that in addition to those forces which are generated from within the planet itself, there is a special type of extra-planetary energy, which emanates from an area of consciousness extraneous to

The Seed of Wisdom

ourselves and our environment. It comprises what we might term the creative or evolutionary energies which express the qualities of the Creator.

We might symbolise this type of energy as high voltage electricity in the sense that it is far too powerful for reception by the receiving centres until it has been 'stepped down' to a lower voltage. To continue the simile, man has in his mechanism what we might term a system of built-in transformers; these are the seven major energy centres in the etheric body. These 'transformers' are, to a certain extent, of variable potential in that at the commencement of a lifetime they will have a pre-determined range of sensitivity which can be increased, within limits, by the efforts of the man himself.

It would seem to be the case that the lower and upper limits of receptivity of the centres in any particular human being is pre-determined by the incarnating soul of that man when equipping himself with his etheric body for the life which he is about to enter. The extent to which the centres with which he equips himself develop their full potential is dependent upon the degree of awareness, and therefore of co-operation between the soul, the dense physical mechanism of manifestation, and the personality in the form of the energy bodies and their centres, which we discussed in the previous chapter on evolution.

In the case of the spiritually undeveloped or average man there will be only a marginal effort at contact

The World of Energies

and the centres will develop only a part of their potential. But in the case of the more highly evolved soul who has achieved a more advanced state in expressing spiritual quality in manifested form, the potential of the centres will probably be extended to their maximum, and possibly at an early stage of that life. This would give the soul the opportunity he is seeking to manifest or express creative energy for a longer period of time than would have been the case had the full potential only been achieved towards the end of that lifetime. We are told that in such cases the soul may even decide to terminate the experience for the purpose of a more rapid advance in the following incarnation, equipped with an etheric body of higher potential which he has now seen that he can handle. This would be the meaning of the Tibetan's statement that death is increasingly due to the Soul's planned intent and planned withdrawal.

But there is another mechanism, which operates on a far higher scale, for 'stepping-down' the high-potential Energies so that they can be registered by humanity for practical purposes. This concerns an aspect of the teaching which it would not be possible even to begin to cover in all its abstruse detail in a short work of this kind, which does not pretend to be more than a very brief introduction to the subject of esotericism. Mention should be made, nevertheless, of this enormously important subject of esoteric astrology, dealing with the vast pattern of projection,

The Seed of Wisdom

transmission and reception of Creative Energy throughout the solar systems of the universe, the planets of our solar system, the energy centres within our planet Earth, within humanity as a whole and finally within man himself.

Astrology is a science which must be restored to its original beauty and truth before the world can gain a truer perspective and a more just and accurate appreciation of the Divine Plan, as it is expressed at this time through the Wisdom of the Ages.

The second statement I would make is that astrology is *essentially* the purest presentation of occult truth in the world at this time, because it is the science which deals with those conditioning and governing energies and forces which play through and upon the whole field of space and all that is found within that field. When this fact is grasped and the sources of those energies are better comprehended . . . the relationships between individual, planetary, systemic and cosmic entities will be grasped, and we shall then begin to live scientifically.

This brings me to the third statement, which is so basic and fundamental that I would ask you to pause and contemplate it, even though you grasp not its full implications as yet. The Ancient Wisdom teaches that 'space is an entity'. It is with the life of this entity, with the forces and energies, the im-

The World of Energies

pulses and the rhythms, the cycles and the times and seasons that esoteric astrology deals.

So, before concentrating on the nature of the energies themselves, let us try to visualise the whole stupendous concept which, as we are told, embraces:

the seven centres of Energy of the One;
the seven streams of energy issuing forth from them;
the seven solar systems of which ours is one;
the seven 'sacred' planets in our solar system;
the seven planetary centres in the etheric body of the planet;
the seven centres of force in the human etheric body;

Esoteric psychology embraces the psychological effect on man, and on humanity as a whole, of the seven streams of force as they affect the whole picture of world conditions. Such a study is the work of a lifetime, but it is being undertaken; and increasingly the trained psychologist will deal with those aspects which are at present esoteric but which will gradually become exoteric as he learns to deal with the causes rather than the effects, with the underlying energies rather than the physical reactions to them.

Again therefore it must be emphasised firstly, that comprehension can only be achieved through the enlightment of the intellect from intuitional – soul – levels of consciousness and, secondly, that the information which follows can be no more than the merest

The Seed of Wisdom

reference to a vast store of knowledge that has been expounded for us, and for future generations, by those Masters who have undertaken the task of guiding humanity into a new area of awareness. For this reason I have no hesitation in quoting freely from the source of the teaching in so far as I am concerned.

The seven streams of energy which we have been discussing have been defined for us as seven major expressions of Divine quality; seven aspects of creative energy emanating from God; and the sum total of the divine Consciousness. As the energies express themselves through form, however subtle such forms may be, the seven rays can also be regarded as seven intelligent Entities through Whom the Plan is working out. Thus They embody, as it were, divine purpose, They 'create the forms through which the divine idea can be carried forward to completion'. So we come to the concept of ray Beings, and perhaps we can dimly envisage, without being specific, the relationship between these Beings and the seven sacred planets of which, we learn, our planet Earth is *not* one.

These seven ray Beings, we are to understand, 'are, unlike man, fully conscious and entirely aware of the purpose and the Plan'. They are 'the sum total of the universal mind' – note universal, not just planetary. Their goal and Their purpose is such, D. K. tells us, that 'it is idle for us to speculate about it, for the highest point of achievement for man is the lowest point for Them.'

The World of Energies

These seven Rays, Breaths and Heavenly Men have the task of wrestling with matter in order to subjugate it to divine purpose, and the goal, as far as one can sense it, is to subject the material forms to the play of the life aspect, thus producing those qualities which will carry the will of God to completion. They are therefore the sum total of all the souls within the solar system and Their activity produces all forms; according to the nature of the form so will be the grade of consciousness.

I am very concerned that this brief excursion into the realms of cosmic and planetary energies should not bring forth from the reader the understandable reaction that all this is 'completely above my head', and therefore of no practical value. Of course it is; in the sense that an understanding of this abstruse concept is above the comprehension of nearly all of us; but not so the distant vision. If we study the practical application to everyday living of the effects of the ray energies; if we endeavour to understand what it is that causes us to react towards each other, and to world conditions, in the way that we do – with the object of trying to react in the way that we *should* – and if in fact we are looking for the causes and not just the effects of all that concerns relationships, we must essentially discover the relationship between the source of the causes and the impact of their effects. It would be unrealistic to start our enterprise by ignoring the

The Seed of Wisdom

cosmic field in which the 'high-voltage' energies arise, and concentrating entirely on the midway point where these energies have already been reduced to the lower voltage potential.

Nevertheless it is equally important that, once having obtained a visionary glimpse of the source and the divine purpose of the Plan in so far as we are able to do so, we should come down to earth, literally and mentally, and direct our efforts towards an understanding of the effects of these seven streams of energy in relation to the physical world, and all that in it lives, for the purpose of manifesting the quality of the consciousness of its Creator. For surely this is indeed the purpose; in much the same way though on an infinitely greater scale, that a lover of beauty – a gardener for instance – would be unlikely to be satisfied by retaining his vision in the mind without expressing it in form; anymore than would a composer be content never to hear the quality of the harmony he had created in his mind.

7
The Seven Rays

THE CONSTITUTION of every human being is subjected to the influence of all the seven rays in varying degrees, but is particularly under the influence of a combination of five of them in varying degree depending upon his stage of spiritual evolution. This is basically what makes one man different from the next. His subtle energy bodies, mental emotional and etheric are, one might say, impregnated with the qualities of the respective rays which condition and control those bodies during that particular incarnation. But the soul itself remains ever under the influence of one particular ray of which it is in fact a part.

A man when in incarnation reacts to the ray of the soul if he is so attuned; and to the rays which are the controlling influences in his three energy bodies; plus, in addition, the ray which takes over the control of the integrated threefold personality at a certain stage of spiritual development. It is at this stage that there begins the struggle between the soul and the personality, which we touched on in Chapter 4, which continues until the natural harmony of the rays is

The Seed of Wisdom

established in the soul-infused personality.

A vast amount of information has been given out in the books of Alice Bailey and the Tibetan Master Djwal Khul on the subject of the seven Rays, presented in a variety of contexts in accordance with the particular branch of the teaching that is under discussion. To reproduce even a fraction of this knowledge on the Rays, given out over a period of thirty years, would be a herculean task, and there would also be the danger that arises, or which certainly can arise, when such esoteric knowledge is taken out of its context. Therefore, such information as is given in this chapter must necessarily be taken from the books, and can constitute no more than an effort to give the reader some idea of the practical implications of the teaching concerning those great energies that condition and, to a large extent, govern our lives.

Perhaps the first thing to do is to circumscribe the subject by listing the Rays, with the names usually ascribed to them, which are to a large extent indicative of the quality they inherently represent; qualities which they can only reflect in man to the extent that they are correctly registered in his consciousness and applied to his activities. Here enters in the factor of the free will of man, which we have discussed earlier, and here too it must be realised that the same energy can be responsible for quite different practical results.

The seven Rays are usually known by the following names:

The Seven Rays

First Ray	of Will or Power.
Second Ray	of Love-Wisdom.
Third Ray	of Active Intelligence or Higher Mind.
Fourth Ray	of Beauty, Harmony and Rhythm.
Fifth Ray	of Concrete Knowledge or Science.
Sixth Ray	of Abstract Idealism.
Seventh Ray	of Ceremonial Order or Organisation.

The first three form a group known as the three Major Rays of Aspect, whilst the other four are known as the Rays of Attribute. The three Major Rays are expressive of the very Essence of the Creator – the Will of God, the Love of God and the Mind of God – to manifest in our solar system as purpose, love-wisdom and intelligence as a result of the impact of these three divine energies on the etheric centres.

The second group comprising the four Rays of Attribute are just as important for the implementation of the Plan, but are said to emphasise in greater detail, and with more specific application to the four kingdoms of nature, certain qualities inherent in the three basic aspects of Creative Will, Love-Wisdom and Intelligence.

It is almost impossible to express in words, but perhaps the reader may be able to grasp the concept

The Seed of Wisdom

intuitively with sufficient clarity to follow the broad outline of this vast and fascinating subject, which will later be seen to have a more practical objective than might at first appear.

The establishment of any Ray energy as a demonstrable quality in the life of the man is largely dependent upon the state of development of some particular centre in the etheric body, the purpose of which is to attract that energy of which in fact it is constituted. It would appear to be the case however, that once registered, that energy will then infuse the whole system with its activity through the interplay and interdependence of all the centres throughout the etheric body.

The energy of the first Ray of Power is registered via the head centre and, as we have already seen in an earlier chapter this centre is fully active only in the very few highly evolved people incarnate in the world today. We can be thankful that this is the case, for imagine the result of a highly developed head centre, responsive to the power of the First Ray of Will in a man in whom there may be little of love-wisdom and who is incapable as yet of building up a balanced personality, nor of registering anything more than self-will and power as an end in itself. History does record such cases, and humanity suffers as a result. 1st Ray energy is the main source of power in all great leaders, dictators and dynamic people who, in most cases, have benefitted mankind; even if many have

The Seven Rays

been misguided or selfish to a degree that has resulted in more harm than good. Much depends upon which of the subtle bodies is controlled by that ray energy, or whether it is the soul that is controlling the life. There are said to be very few 1st ray souls in incarnation, for the very reason mentioned above; but when they do incarnate, such souls are likely to leave a very definite impression. It may be the case that a soul has deliberately chosen to acquire a mental body of 1st Ray energy for the express purpose of a dynamic demonstration of – let us say – the soul quality of love and wisdom. This would be more likely to arise in the case of a most highly evolved soul, experienced to the degree of being able to 'select', or to 'attract', for the ensuing incarnation energy 'substance' of a quality suitable for building up a personality for a definite objective. The difficulty would then arise when the inevitable struggle would take place between the soul and the personality, which would at first resist domination by the soul; and if the self-will of the powerful 1st ray mental body, and perhaps the whole personality should fail to respond to the purpose of the indwelling soul, the experiment would be a failure and that particular experience would be frustrated.

It is not the purpose to fill this chapter with information on the seven rays as an end in itself, although it is a fascinating subject; but to give the reader an opportunity to let his mind dwell on these matters as part of a general appreciation of the whole underlying

The Seed of Wisdom

pattern of energies which is the cause of behaviourism. Generalisations, just as much as particular aspects, must be approached with caution; but nevertheless a certain amount of the information available from the teaching may be helpful, even at this stage, for an understanding of the world of energies.

To return to the subject of the 1st Ray of Will or Power, it would be, I think, correct to say that whilst this dynamic energy is comparatively seldom manifested as a soul quality, it is increasingly becoming an important influence in the personality, and particularly the mental expression of the more highly evolved man, as the head centre becomes more active.

With reference to what has been said earlier regarding the soul and personality of a Nation, it is pertinent to mention that both Great Britain and Germany are regarded as 1st Ray *personalities*; whilst India and China are 1st Ray *souls*. Great Britain has a *soul* on the 2nd Ray of Love-Wisdom. Much understanding can result from a study of these ray characteristics in the Nations.

The second of the rays of aspect, the Ray of Love – Wisdom brings – in that divine quality which it is essential for humanity to assimilate and express before it can be entrusted with the power of the first ray. It is the present purpose of humanity to express this quality, and this of course was the message of the Christ. It would probably be true to say that although the influence of this ray is often manifested through

The Seven Rays

the personality bodies, it is primarily a soul energy, and increasingly more 2nd Ray souls are coming into incarnation. Unfortunately this does not mean that the essence of pure love automatically will penetrate to practical living, for this depends on a number of factors. It depends, in the first place, on the evolution, or perhaps we should say the activity, of the etheric heart centre in humanity, for it is through this centre that the energy of the 2nd Ray is registered. When the heart centre in a man is relatively inactive, as it is in millions of human beings, 2nd Ray energy passes on to the solar plexus centre where it registers as desire – desire for things that are attractive to the personal self. After all, love is essentially attraction, and it manifests under the Law of Attraction in every kingdom of nature. It demonstrates as desire for contact, for different motives at different levels of consciousness; from the sex instinct all the way up to spiritual devotion, to soul awareness, soul contact, soul-personality fusion; and then finally it leads to the realisation that all is really One.

Wisdom, which is the other quality of the 2nd Ray has been described by the Tibetan as intelligent love. The hall-mark of humanity is intelligence; it is intelligence that distinguishes man from the animals, and it is intelligence that distills love from desire. This is why a second condition is required for the full manifestation of love by humanity, which is response to the 3rd Ray of Intelligence or Higher Mind.

The Seed of Wisdom

But let us hear what the Tibetan has to say about the characteristics of a man on the 2nd Ray of Love-Wisdom in Alice Bailey's book, A Treaty on the Seven Rays, VOL. I:

> This is called the ray of wisdom for its characteristic desire for pure knowledge and for absolute truth – cold and selfish if without love, and inactive without power. When both power and love are present, then you have the ray of the Buddhas and of all great teachers of humanity – those who, having attained wisdom for the sake of others, spend themselves in giving it forth.
>
> The second ray man will have tact and foresight; he will make an excellent ambassador, and a first rate teacher or head of a college; as a man of affairs, he will have clear intelligence and wisdom in dealing with matters which come before him, and he will have the capacity of impressing true views of things on others and of making them see things as he does. He will make a good business man, if modified by the fourth, fifth and seventh rays.

On the other hand D. K. speaks of mis-interpretations of the energy of this ray, which man can manifest in the form of over-absorption in study, coldness, indifference to others and contempt of the mental limitations of others.

A bad type of the 2nd ray would be bent on acquiring knowledge for himself alone, absolutely

The Seven Rays

indifferent to the human needs of others. The foresight of such a man would degenerate into suspicion, his calmness into coldness and hardness of nature.

So we see that the mere fact of being under the influence of this great ray energy of Love-Wisdom is of itself alone no passport to perfection; time, effort and intelligence are essential.

The 3rd Ray of Active Intelligence or Higher Mind finds its expression through the etheric throat centre in the spiritually evolved man. It is the energy of this major ray which, when working as soul energy in conjunction with a personality composed of certain other ray qualities, can produce the brilliant intellectual. 'It is the ray of the abstract thinker, the ray of the philosopher, the metaphysician and the higher mathematician. When the 5th ray of concrete knowledge or science is the secondary ray influence in conjunction with the 3rd ray, we get the great scientific geniuses; whilst the combination of 3rd ray energy with the 4th ray of beauty and harmony may produce the great composer.

Nations that have 3rd ray personalities are France and China. France, with a fifth ray soul and 3rd ray personality demonstrates the intellectual brilliance that can result from this combination and, as Alice Bailey says in her book The Destiny of the Nations, when the intellect of the French is turned towards the discovery and the elucidation of the things of the

The Seed of Wisdom

spirit, instead of living in the wonder of their past glory as an empire, then they will carry revelation to the world. The spiritual potential of China is of the greatest significance, with a 1st ray soul combined with a personality controlled by the 3rd ray of Higher Mind.

The first of the 4 minor rays of attribute is the 4th Ray of Beauty or Harmony, frequently called the ray of Harmony through Conflict; a curious paradox at first sight but not after deeper consideration. Conflict does in fact lead to harmony; and in the struggle which eventually takes place between the integrated personality and the indwelling soul, this 4th ray is of paramount importance. It is one of the three rays which, at some stage of a man's development, must govern the mental body and determine his personality. We are told that its effect is to emphasise the basic quality of the 2nd Ray of love, bringing out the virtues of sympathy, generosity, strong affections and devotion; but also physical courage and quickness of intellect and perception. It is also the ray of colour and the artist; and of melody and the musician. Wrongly interpreted it can result in self-centredness, worrying, lack of moral (but not physical) courage, strong passions, indolence and extravagance. It will not therefore come as a surprise to learn that it is one of the most powerful ray energies affecting humanity today.

The other ray of attribute strongly affecting humanity is the 5th Ray of Concrete Knowledge and

The Seven Rays

Science, concerned with the evolution of the mental body or lower mind, as distinguished from Higher Mind or soul consciousness. In the more highly evolved type of man, this ray operates through the ajna centre, the etheric centre between the eyebrows. It results, in the words of The Treatise on the Seven Rays, in a keen sense of justice, strict accuracy, perseverance, uprightness, common sense and keen intellect. It is the ray of science and research, as its name implies, but nonetheless, when wrongly applied it can produce narrow mindedness, arrogance and prejudice.

> The attribute of concrete knowledge whereby man is enabled to concretise his concepts and so build thoughtforms whereby he materialises his visions and his dreams and brings his ideas into being. This he does through the activity of the lower concrete mind.

The 6th Ray of Idealism and Devotion, acting through the solar plexus centre, is responsible for much of the idealism, religious fervour and intense personal feeling that humanity has been demonstrating throughout our historical age. It is the ray of the mystic and the saint, but also of the religious fanatic and inquisitor. Both Spain and Italy have the 6th Ray as their soul ray, and of these two, Italy has the 4th Ray of Harmony through Conflict as the personality ray whereas, in contrast, Spain is on the personality ray

[75]

The Seed of Wisdom

of Ceremonial Order – the 7th Ray of attribute. Certainly it would appear that the characteristics of nations are more easily discernable as a result of the rays that influence them, than is the case when we attempt an analysis of a human being – especially when we try to establish our own ray influences.

In relation to the name of this 6th ray, it should be observed that the term 'devotion' relates, not only to personal devotion and religious worship but also, we are told, it includes man's devotion to his ideas, ideals and vision as he moves forward, 'according to the depths of his discontent as he passes from one stage of temporary satisfaction to another', along the path towards union with his soul and then with Spirit.

From the science of esoteric astrology we learn that due to the juxtaposition of certain sacred planets in relation to the Earth, the influence of the 6th ray, so dominant during the past 2000 years, is now waning as we pass from the Piscean Age to the Age of Aquarius, bringing into activity the 7th Ray which will increasingly influence humanity during the next 2000 years. An incursion into the mysteries of Zodiacal influences would be quite out of place here, even if the writer could attempt such a venture into the realm of astrology, which is unfortunately not the case. But this need not divert us from our purpose of emphasising the importance of this transition from 6th ray influence to that of the 7th ray, and its significance in relation to world affairs as we find them at the present time.

The Seven Rays

As a result of this 7th ray influence man will develop increased group consciousness and will move away from *individual* self awareness. The emphasis will be on relationship in every sphere of activity; between nations and between races; within and between groups, in which there will be a more equal spread of authority. There will be a tendency to break away from the older pattern of people gathered around a leader, and this may well be the cause of the present rebellion against central authority, particularly by youth, for the young are more likely to be receptive to the new energy that is gradually replacing the outgoing 6th ray with its emphasis on personal devotion.

The 7th ray, through its impact on the sacral centre of the human being, may well be the underlying cause of the present day manifestation of uncontrolled sex activity; for this is the ray that governs the sex relation in all the kingdoms of nature.

The greatest benefit to be derived from the increasing influence of 7th ray energy over the next 2000 years of the Aquarian Age will be, we are told, enhanced awareness of the soul-personality relationship; whilst the great hope for the future lies in the possibility of group endeavour eventually to eliminate extreme nationalism, and intolerance in religious matters, all leading to the goal of world government and a world religion. Above all, this change from personal idealism, so necessary for progress in the past age, to 7th ray relationship and rhythm, underlines the

The Seed of Wisdom

importance of personality integration, so that the personality as a whole can respond intelligently to its particular ray purpose in harmony with the purpose of the soul.

Here we must end this very short dissertation on the Seven Rays; intended for no other purpose than to round-out the readers' vision of the vast field of energies that underlies and is the cause of the world of appearances. It is in no sense whatever intended to expound the teaching on the Seven Rays, which requires years of study and thought and meditation; and which, in any case, can only be properly expounded by a Master of the Wisdom; and then even They express the impossibility of communicating Their knowledge to man in his present state of spiritual unpreparedness. For those whose interest has been aroused, the books of Alice Bailey and the Tibetan Master are the key to knowledge, and in particular the five volumes of A Treatise on the Seven Rays.

To end this chapter I quote below an excerpt from the Tibetan's writings selected from these books by The Group for Creative Meditation at Sundial House, Tunbridge Wells:

Students at this time would do well to remember that all basic changes taking place upon the physical plane are necessarily the result of inner subjective causes, emanating from some level of the divine consciousness, and therefore from some plane other than the physical. The fact that tremendous and unusual upheavals are taking place in the kingdoms of nature is attributed by men to other men or to certain forces generated by human thinking, frailty and ambition ... The significance of the present happenings is intepreted (and necessarily so) in terms of human awareness and responsiveness ... whereas that is not basically so. Humanity suffers and experiences as a result of the inner occurrencies and the meeting of subjective forces and inflowing energies.

There is a line of descending energy which has its origin outside our planetary life altogether; the inflow of this energy, its inevitable effect under cyclic law and its consequences, as they work out upon the physical plane, has produced and is producing all the changes of which mankind is so terribly aware at this time. This swings into immediate conflict the past and the future, and in this statement I have expressed the deepest esoteric truth which mankind is competent to grasp ...

8
On Meditation

MOST GENUINE esoteric schools devote their activities to three inter-related fields of endeavour, which are knowledge, meditation and service.

It must, I think, be reiterated here that the acquisition of knowledge in these matters is a means to an end, and not an end in itself; it will profit us little if the motive is idle curiosity. The objective towards which we are moving becomes clearer as the inevitable expansion in consciousness takes place and we are enabled to sense the vision. It must be obvious that if we propose to invoke the wisdom and spiritual will-to-good of the higher mind, for the purpose of co-operating to the best of our ability in a divine plan which we sense may give a deeper meaning to life, we must first gain an understanding, however incomplete, of that plan and of what may lie behind the world of appearances. Hence the necessity for spiritual knowledge.

Meditation is the means, or one of the means, of contacting the world in which this deeper meaning to life is to be found; by bridging the gap in consciousness between the Self and the not-self, between the man in

On Meditation

physical incarnation and the indwelling soul; between lower and higher mind.

Service in this context is service to the plan, and service to the plan involves every field of activity that advances the process of evolution. Therefore meditation is service; the understanding and practice of right human relations is service, as is also all that gives us insight into the underlying causes of the problems of humanity with a view to playing our part, however small, in alleviating them.

No matter how far you go in the scale of Being, you will find – from the fourth kingdom onward – that the technique of meditation governs all expansion of consciousness, all registration of the Plan or Purpose and, in fact, the entire process of evolutionary unfoldment. It is a technique of spiritual apprehension, of focussing attention on some level of consciousness or other, and also of originating contacts.

It might also be stated that it is meditation that is responsible for transforming the desire of the ordinary human being into spiritual will.

Meditation is not a substitute for prayer, but rather is it an extension of prayer, introducing mental effort at a time when man is shifting his focus of consciousness from emotional levels to those of the mind. Michal Eastcott expresses this admirably in her book The Silent Path. She says:

The Seed of Wisdom

In the past prayer was the great life-line providing the link with what was felt to be Reality. It was the refuge turned to in adversity and danger, the method by which aid was entreated. It was the comfort of the needy, the strength of the fearful. It was also a true magnetic channel, for it tied the supplicant in with the greater powers to which he was appealing, and along that 'life-line' energy flowed.

Prayer – using the word in its specific sense – is also characterised by feeling, and people are today seeking to use their minds to approach Reality. They have learnt to distrust feeling. Prayer remains, therefore, a foundation for approach to the inner realms, but upon its up-turning attitude we superimpose meditation and gain the co-operation of the mind. We thus approach the unknown or superconscious areas with intelligence as well as desire.

Prayer is still the comfort of the needy and the strength of the fearful, and millions of people in every part of the world have yet to reach that state of mental development that will enable them to make use of the more mental approach. Many of them require, and will continue to require, a simple and almost childlike faith in an individual God in human likeness who will listen to their personal appeals for material and specific help in adversity; and who will personally preside over a heaven where, at the end of their lives

On Meditation

they may find eternal rest. They also require places of worship where they can find peace and quiet and solace, human companionship and love, and a refuge from the turmoil of their daily lives. All this, and more, is provided by the orthodox churches of every religion; and without their discipline and spiritual care for the as yet unevolved masses, as well as for the average educated man, the trend towards selfishness, greed and unthinking materialism would be difficult to arrest. This is the problem of the churches in the more developed countries of the world – how to provide for the need of those millions of people not yet prepared for the more mental approach to divinity, without losing the support of those who are seeking something more. Perhaps this is what Djwal Khul wanted to convey in his words:

> I would like to pause at this point and ask you to remember that I refer *not* here to religious meditation, strictly understood or those invocative appeals for help which are so closely associated in the minds of the western Christian thinker. I refer to all who – in quiet reflection, focussed appeal and with a true background of knowledge – are able to 'think through' into a higher state of consciousness than the one of which we are normally aware.

So meditation is not a substitute for church but is, as Michal Eastcott has said, a technique that we can superimpose on our more orthodox religious affiliations

The Seed of Wisdom

– whatever they may be – and so enrich our spiritual experience.

The essence of all religions is faith; prayer is the method of approach in the form of an appeal to divinity through the higher emotions. The meditative approach also requires faith – faith in ourselves as soul – infused personalities capable of invoking a response from the spiritual levels within ourselves. We ask, in meditation, nothing for the separate self – or rather not-self – except the light of understanding that will kill out the illusion of our separateness as we attempt to open up the channel of consciousness between the personality and the soul and to register that contact in the phyiscal brain.

The practice of meditation is acquired by degrees. At first it is a discipline, and all disciplines require effort. The man who is mentally evolved is accustomed to concentration, but he is usually concentrating his mind on some problem that he finds absorbing. It is not quite so easy to concentrate the mind, as an act of will, on something that at that particular moment is not absorbing. A friend of mine once said that he found it distressing, when in church, to find that his mind was pre-occupied with whether he had left the front door open; and it is quite extraordinary how difficult it is to sit down and deliberately concentrate for five minutes on a chosen subject not related to our immediate desire. Still more difficult, and quite pointless as well, is to attempt to shut off the entire

On Meditation

process of thought and 'make the mind a blank'. As we shall see later, this is *not* the state of mind for meditation.

This meditation on a chosen subject is known as reflective meditation. We can choose any subject in the beginning, when disciplining the lower mind, but obviously it is preferable to choose a subject on which, at a later stage, the higher mind can make a contribution. We might choose just a word, like 'compassion' or 'love', or perhaps even 'energy' in the sense that we have been considering spiritual energy in the earlier chapters. Or we might choose a phrase or dictum such as, for example, 'energy follows thought' or 'as a man thinketh in his heart, so is he': or perhaps 'man is a soul and he has a body'. Now we can begin to see why esoteric knowledge must accompany meditation – to provide a fertile soil for the reception of further knowledge which we plan to invoke from the higher source.

This brings us to the next type of meditation, which is without a seed thought, and is usually known as receptive meditation. This is a rather more advanced stage and is very much more difficult. Without a seed-thought the mind is far more free to roam, and it is at this stage that we face the problem of keeping the mind free and yet active. Michal Eastcott, in her book already quoted, uses the term 'thought-free consciousness'. In the earlier stages of this form of meditation it is probably as well to have a chosen subject in mind, but without giving it such definite form as we do in

The Seed of Wisdom

reflective meditation. It is at this stage that we begin the work of bridging the gap in consciousness between the personality, the soul and Higher Mind, for which we need the ability to visualise, and to make use of symbols without allowing them to materialise into anything more than an aid to our understanding.

For example we can visualise the Spiritual Triad as the Monad, or Spirit of man reflecting the three aspects of Divinity – Spiritual Will or Purpose, Love – Wisdom, and Higher Mind. Then we visualise the three aspects of the soul, as the vehicle of Spirit embodying these same energies for transmission to the personality, expressed again symbolically as a triangle of the mental, emotional and etheric bodies underlying the dense physical body of man. Then we try to visualise our consciousness reaching out towards the higher levels as we attempt to build the bridge between the brain and the lower mind, which is the highest aspect of the personality, and the soul; and then between the soul-infused personality and Higher Mind, which is the lowest aspect of the Monad or Spiritual Triad.

Symbolically it might be expressed thus: (see the diagram opposite).

It is not suggested that one should attempt a form of meditation such as the above until experience has been gained and the mind can be held steady, and free of the inconsequential thoughts that continually flutter in and disturb the serenity and concentration.

On Meditation

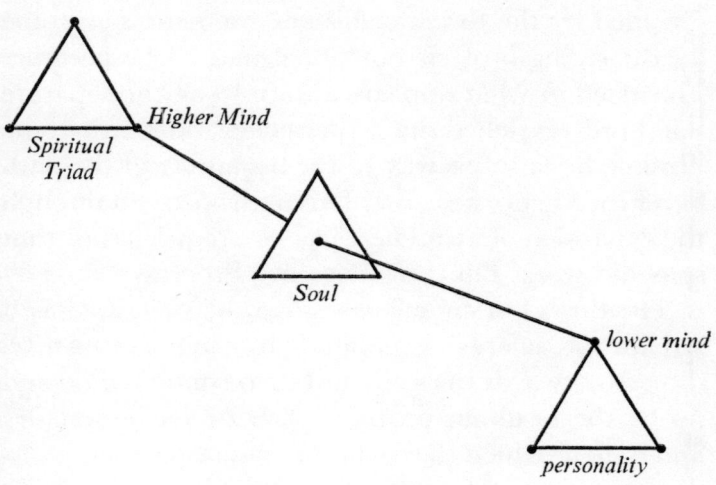

Nevertheless the example may possibly give some idea of the process, and this particular example may start up a line of thought or meditation on the thread of consciousness which leads man back from the 'dense material world into the Spiritual'.

Man – the whole man and not just the physical vehicle – comes into being through the down-pouring vital energy of the One Life of which we are a part. The stream of life pouring *through* the soul is 'anchored' in the heart, and is the so-called silver thread of life, which in the eastern teaching is termed the Sutratma. The physical man seems to be, as it were,

The Seed of Wisdom

overwhelmed by the experience of manifestation. Gripped by the forces of his environment, overcome by the strength of his emotional nature, he becomes immersed in what appears to him to be the separate self until, enriched by experience and sensing the illusion, he finds his way to the beginning of the path of return whence he came. This path opens up through the expansion of awareness. We are reminded of that splendid work, Bunyan's Pilgrim's Progress.

The thread of consciousness can be visualised as a stream of energy generated by the *personality*, directed towards the soul, and then continued on and up by the resultant partnership between personality and soul, in which the soul is the senior partner.

> the new and true science of the mind which will utilise mental substance for the building of the bridges between personality and soul and then between the soul and the spiritual triad. This constitutes active work in subtler substance than the substance of the three worlds of normal evolution. It concerns the substance of the three higher levels of the mental plane. These symbolic bridges, when constructed, will facilitate the stream or flow of consciousness and produce that continuity of consciousness, of that sense of unimpeded awareness which will finally end the fear of death, negate all sense of separateness, and make a man responsive in his brain consciousness to impressions coming to

On Meditation

him from the higher spiritual realms or from the mind of God. He will be more easily initiated into the purposes and plans of the Creator.

The symbolic representation of the three levels of consciousness depicted by the triangles could be used for daily reflective meditation, in which, for a while, we would ponder deeply on all its possible meanings and implications, using mainly for this purpose the intellect and our slowly accumulating knowledge. Then again, it could be used for receptive meditation as a setting in which the lower mind would be held in a state of 'thought-free consciousness' for impression from the higher level of consciousness. Finally it could be used, as could of course any other symbol, for invocation. This is an extension of meditation in which we seek to invoke, by an effort of will, a response from the higher level as we attempt to build these symbolic bridges into the world of Spirit.

Dr. Roberto Assagioli, the author of Psychosynthesis, has this to say on invocation:

> it includes and combines the use of all our inner functions. It is a simultaneous activity of the mind (meditation), of feeling (prayer), of the imagination (visualisation), and of the will (affirmation). It is obvious that this comprehensive and synthesised action of our whole being, when rightly carried out, gives to invocation a potency incomparably greater

and richer than the separate use of any single inner activity.

From The Silent Path

The last type of meditation we shall consider is termed Creative Meditation. This, in the last analysis, is the cause of our very being; yet though it is the medium through which the Creator implements His Plan, we can participate in creative meditation, in however humble degree, by our contribution in opening up the channel of consciousness, which in eastern terms is known as the Antahkarana. Through this medium, not only can the ideas from higher sources be impressed upon the mind via the soul, right through to the brain consciousness, but by our efforts the resultant thought-forms can be impulsed out into the world in the form of ideals for constructive action in every field of human endeavour.

A thought is given; a symbol described; an idea portrayed. Then as the minds of men ponder upon it and the intuitives of the world pick up the thought, it serves as a seed-thought which eventually comes to fruition with the presentation and the unfolding of a revelation which serves to lead the race of men nearer to their goal.

There comes a time, far ahead for most of us, when the fully integrated man is able to hold the mind actively poised and spiritually orientated, without at

On Meditation

the same time withdrawing his attention from the work that needs to be done in the world around him in which he lives. This is what Djwal Khul describes as the dual life of the disciple:

> This involves a dual activity; the lower mind becomes a potent factor in directing the service activities of the disciple. These activities become the major motivating potency in the disciple's life and are a consequence of a growing soul fusion with the personality, thus developing and unfolding his sense of inclusiveness. Inclusiveness is the supreme key to the understanding of consciousness. At the same time the higher mind is impressing the lower mind and drawing it into a higher fusion with itself.

Here we must conclude what is intended as only the briefest commentary on the nature and general objectives of meditation. For a deeper understanding of the science – for a science it is – there is a wealth of literature available from very many quite different sources. From the East we have those marvellous works, the Upanishads written between 800 and 400 B. C., highly mystical, of which Juan Mascaró writes:

> These compositions are as much above the mere archaeological curiosity of some scholars as light is above its definition. Scholarship is necessary to bring us the fruits of ancient wisdom, but only an elevation of thought and emotion can help us to enjoy them and transform them into life.

The Seed of Wisdom

Then we have the writings of the saints and mystics of the East and West, too numerous to mention, but mainly expressing the devotional path of the mystic rather than the equally important path of the mind, with which we are concerned in this introduction to esotericism. We have the books of Alice A. Bailey and the Tibetan Master Dwjal Khul impregnated by the theme of meditation, which is the very essence of the teaching of the Ageless Wisdom. Her two volumes of Discipleship in the New Age are a revelation of the modern relationship between a Master of the Wisdom and his disciples; they are not only highly instructive and full of spiritual meaning, they are also deeply moving. Other books of A. A. B. which are particularly orientated towards the science of meditation are, From Intellect to Intuition, Letters on Occult Meditation, and The Light of the Soul.

But before embarking on these rather more difficult treatises on meditation and the whole science of esotericism, many may find Michal Eastcott's splendid introduction to the subject – The Silent Path – exactly what they are looking for.

9
Practical Application

IT IS fashionable these days to say that 'God is dead'; that no progress is being made towards the higher ideals of civilisation, and to point out that the rich are getting richer and the poor are getting poorer; whilst the hall-mark of this affluent society is materialism. Though some of this may be true to some extent, it ignores the progress that has been made, and it is the cry of those who have lost their faith in humanity and in themselves. One of the reasons for this despondency is the failure to apply the right time scale to the slow process of evolution and social progress. It is no use to compare each decade with the previous decade nor one generation with the preceding one. Even periods as comparatively long as centuries are short in the history of a nation or a race, and in the context of world evolution, they are very short indeed.

One has only to look back to the state of the world 500 years ago and seriously to consider conditions in which all but the privileged few in every country were then living, to recognise progress. People are inclined to concentrate on the appalling atrocities that have taken place in the last century, the horror of

The Seed of Wisdom

the world wars and civil strife, and the disregard for human rights. But evolution does not proceed smoothly, nor is the process of change always humane. We are prone to forget slavery and child-labour, civil wars and inquisitions, persecutions, pograms and religious crusades; and canabilism was quite common in some countries which today are members of the community of nations.

We tend to associate ourselves with the age in which we live, and our concepts of progress, or lack of it, are strongly affected by myopia despite our knoweldge of history. Perhaps if we were able to realise that we, as souls, have played a part in that history, and will again play a part in the history of the future, not only might we see things in a different perspective, but we might be more inclined to prepare for active participation in a future not limited to a single lifetime of which a large part is spent in equipping ourselves with the bare essentials for an intelligent existence.

There have been in the past, and there are today, many saints and mystics in the world, some of whom are quite unaware of their saintliness. There are many thousands of men and women of goodwill who are consciously or unconsciously alive to their spiritual, as distinct from their practical, responsibilities in the fields of government, education and religion. Hundreds of thousands of men and women of every nationality, colour and creed are concerned with the approach to divinity, or with the needs of humanity,

Practical Application

or with both. A very great number of those who work in the fields of philosophy, psychology, sociology, medicine, biology, capital-labour relations, and finance have a keen sense of their contribution to the growth of spiritual values and the evolution of mankind. These are the men and women, professional and non-professional, but essentially intelligent and sensitive, who over the next 2000 years will have the task of awakening the latent sense of divinity and the will-to-good in the teeming millions who are still unaware of any purpose to life other than the necessity to live in a state that is conducive to the maximum of physical comfort obtainable for themselves and their immediate families and associates, regardless of the needs of others.

It is on these more or less integrated personalities, many of whom are beginning to be soul conscious, that the Hierarchy of Perfected Souls – the Masters of the Wisdom – will continue to depend for the implementation of the ideas and ideals which They, under the leadership of the Christ – the Master of all the Masters – intuit through their illumed minds from that even higher Spiritual Centre which is beyond the direct comprehension of man. It is through the intelligent sensitivity to these ideas and ideals that man arrives at 'an awareness of requirements and the ability to bring together the need and that which is required to meet that need'; and this is the reason why the Tibetan Master, in the introduction to the book *Discipleship*

The Seed of Wisdom

in the New Age, describes World Service as:

1. Intuitional response to ideas.
2. Sensitiveness to the impression which some member of the Hierarchy may seek to make upon the mind of the disciple.
3. Quick response to real need.
4. Right observation of reality upon the soul plane, which leads to right mental perception, to freedom from illusion and to the illumination of the brain.
5. Correct manipulation of force, involving therefore an understanding of the types and qualities of force and their right creative weaving into service upon the outer plane.
6. A true comprehension of the time element with its cyclic ebb and flow and the right seasons for action.

Do we now begin to understand why, under this particular school of thought, for the comprehension of what is required of us, and therefore what is the purpose of life, it has been necessary to explain the fundamentals of the Ageless Wisdom teaching concerning the etheric body, the world of energies and the seven rays, the doctrine of re-birth, and the existence of the Hierarchy?

If this is the case then, The Tibetan tells us, the first thing we have to do is to acquire the quality of 'mental

Practical Application

polarisation' which, he says, must express itself in two ways:

1. Through the life of meditation.
2. Through the control of the astral body.

Increasingly must your inner life be lived upon the mental plane. Steadily and without descent must the attitude of meditation be held – not for a few minutes each morning . . . but constantly all day long. It infers a constant orientation to life and the handling of life from the angle of the soul. This does not refer to what is so often referred to as 'turning one's back upon the world'. The disciple faces the world but he faces it from the level of the soul, looking clear eyed upon the world of human affairs.

Increasingly must the normal and powerful life of the emotional, astral, desire and glamorous nature be controlled and rendered quiescent by the life of the soul, functioning through the mind. The emotions which are normally self-centred and personal must be transmuted into the realisations of universality and impersonality; the astral body must become the organ through which the love of the soul can pour; desire must give place to aspiration and that, in its turn, must be merged in the group life and the group good . . . the pure light of the mind must pour into all the dark places of the lower nature. These are the results of mental polarisation and

The Seed of Wisdom

are brought about by definite meditation and the cultivation of the meditative attitude.

The achievement of a constantly held attitude of meditation and the resultant soul consciousness, whilst at the same time continuing to live and enjoy an 'earthly' life of practical usefulness and happiness amongst friends and relations, is of course the aim of all who have found their way to the beginning of the Path; but few would hope to fulfil this distant vision of near-perfection, relatively speaking, at the present time. Yet a start can be made once we understand the purpose, and I have reproduced the above statement by the Tibetan because of its most inclusive phrasing. The emphasis on mental polarisation is paramount and practical; and no student of esotericism, no aspirant to discipleship would fail to recognise the need to bring the emotional nature under mental control. Indeed, this is basic in all systems of education and training. But note also, that there is no suggestion that we need be discouraged by the strength of our emotional nature and the difficulty of bringing it under control. An absence of tenderness, of sensitivity to others, of warmth and enthusiasm for life is surely something to regret and, if possible, to be remedied. But of course the more powerful the emotional nature, the more difficult it is to bring it under mental control – and the more satisfactory. It is rather like the horseman who finds little satisfaction in controlling a

Practical Application

dispirited and unresponsive creature and longs for the opportunity to handle a thoroughbred; and so the harnessing of a powerful astral body can be a joy to the seeker on the path towards soul consciousness.

The dual sense of awareness, which is to be aware in the brain of a higher sense of consciousness – that of the soul – has been the aim of many schools of philosophical thought and training. A reflection on what we call 'absent mindedness', or action without thought, may result in the realisation that this is a lower form of intelligent action without spiritual purpose. Obviously not all intelligent action requires spiritual purpose but, for so many of us, no action of ours has any conscious soul motivation.

There have been several exponents of the theory or doctrine that average man is only half awake, and that the uncoordinated dream experience is, in comparison with his waking state, somewhat similar to the latter state of awareness when compared with consciousness which results from the soul illumed intellect. Both P. D. Ouspensky and Gudjieff expounded this doctrine, and gave training in the expansion of awareness, and Dr. Roberto Assagioli, the founder of the doctrine of Psycho-synthesis, goes further, in the establishment of a programme to build a new personality around the nucleus of the mental complex that has been awakened through meditation.

It is necessary to say something here about the use of the word 'disciple', lest it should be thought

The Seed of Wisdom

presumptuous to use a term that is usually associated with the Disciples of Christ. The word disciple is defined in the dictionary as 'one who receives the teaching of another; a follower'. The Disciples of Christ, 2000 years ago, were very much more than this, in that they did literally give up all to follow Him, and were taught at first hand by a Teacher, or Master of the Wisdom, in full physical manifestation Who produced in them that mystical devotion which at that time and in that Age was the key to illumination. But many are aspirants to discipleship which, in the context of the teaching expounded by the Tibetan, means integration into the group of men and women who are alive and sensitive to the ideas and ideals that the Hierarchy is striving to implant in the minds of men; by opening up a channel of communication between the world of men in physical incarnation and the world of souls wherein are to be found, not only the souls of those men, but also the Hierarchy of perfected Souls that we call the Masters of the Wisdom. Receiving, or trying to receive to the best of our ability, the teaching of the Hierarchy, and to carry it out in practice, to the extent that we are able to do so, is what we mean by discipleship in this Age; and there need be nothing presumptuous in this aspiration.

In speaking of the various sub-groups within the one group of aspirants and disciples, the Tibetan has this to say:

The seed groups are organised to provide channels

Practical Application

in the world for the distribution of certain peculiar types of force which will work out into manifestation in specific ways ... I refer to the energies used in relation to the awakening of the human consciousness, to the integration of the world of souls with the world of men. I refer to the activities whereby the human kingdom can become a great station of light and a powerhouse of spiritual force, distributing it to the other kingdoms in nature ... This manipulation of energies has for centuries been carried forward by us (the Hierarchy) but its effects have only been registered unconsciously by man ... Now it has seemed to us possible to focus the light and knowledge much more definitely and to form groups on earth composed of the isolated responding individuals – so that more light and more knowledge can be spread abroad.

These groups are already functioning, as super-consciousness in man is added to his hitherto normal states of consciousness and sub-consciousness, and this is why earlier reference was made to saints and mystics and men and women of goodwill who either *consciously*, because of their spiritual sensitivity; or *unconsciously*, through the impact of the ray energies on the etheric centres, are alive to their responsibilities in fields of endeavour such as government, education and religion. In all fields of endeavour man is increasingly becoming more conscious of the underlying

The Seed of Wisdom

purpose of his activities, and it would seem that increasingly the youth of this present generation is seeking more than just monetary reward in the choice of their life work.

Another distinctive feature of the spiritual evolution of man in the coming age which has just commenced, consists in the absence of imposed authority. There is no demand for obedience and no threat of punishment as in the past.

> I will teach you (Says the Tibetan Master). Whether or not you profit by the teaching is entirely your own affair; that is something that the disciples of the new Age need to learn ... In the olden days in the East, the Master exacted from His disciple that implicit obedience which actually made the Master responsible and placed upon His shoulders the destiny or the karma of the disciple. That condition no longer holds good. The intellectual principle in the individual is now too much developed to warrant this type of expectancy ... in the coming Age, the Master is responsible for the offering of opportunity and for the right enunciation of the truth but for no more than that.

He then tells his disciples that one basic essential is required, and that is 'a persevering earnestness which nothing will deter'.

Most teaching and training related to spiritual matters is formulated through what are generally

Practical Application

termed Laws and Principles, which lend themselves to a number of interpretations according to the level at which they are to be implemented. The so-called Laws of Nature can be seen to be one particular aspect of these Laws and Principles as relating to dense physical forms, whether Universal, Planetary, or to any one or to all of the four Kingdoms of Nature – mineral, vegetable, animal, or human. These Laws are immutable, and in most cases they can be seen to be so, as for example in the case of the law of gravity. But the pull of gravity, which we term weight, is a part of the Law of Attraction, and another aspect of the same Law is demonstrated by the fact that living beings gravitate towards each other, or repel one another, in much the same way as we observe in the positive or negative force exerted in a magnetic field. Physical and emotional love is another manifestation of the same Law of Attraction, and in this particular manifestation it affects the behaviour of human personalities. It may be an instinctual manifestation as in the case of the animals or savage man, or it may be emotional as in the case of average man. The Commandments enunciated by Moses to the Israelites formulated the Law of Attraction in a number of injunctions or rules concerning mans' relation to God, and to his neighbour. The Christ extended these concepts in an effort to teach man the real meaning of love, as distinct from a set of rules; but He was still dealing with the personality level of love. These

The Seed of Wisdom

concepts became imbedded in Christian ethics. But in His Parables there was a far deeper esoteric meaning, which was hidden in the sense that man was not yet capable of a full realisation of the meaning of Love.

Alice Bailey, in her foreword to the book, Discipleship in the New Age, refers to 'a growing responsiveness to contacts and to individuals of which the average human being knows nothing'.

Elsewhere, the Tibetan points out that the attitude of thought for the well-being of others is at present an effort, and He invites us to give thought to what the world would be like if, without effort, and always, we considered the interests of others rather than our own. This can be seen as yet another extension of the Law of Attraction to include group consciousness in the sense of inclusive love for our fellow men instead of for ourselves.

The point to grasp is that all of the so called Laws and Principles of the Wisdom teaching and training can be interpreted as applicable at the purely dense-physical level, when they are more commonly called the Laws of Nature; or they can be applied at the personality level, when they are the basis of ethics and morality; or they can be expounded from the angle of the soul as man becomes capable, through meditation and mental polarisation, of bringing into his physical brain consciousness the purpose of the indwelling soul. This is the purpose of the esoteric schools and of many groups which exist all over the world today; to bring into our field of awareness, knowledge concerning the

Practical Application

existence of the Hierarchy of Masters as They seek to guide the evolution of mankind; knowledge of the energies and forces that control our destiny, knowledge of the soul and the doctrine of re-birth; and wisdom to apply this knowledge to the best ends.

Once more it is necessary to emphasise that this brief introduction to esotericism and the Ageless Wisdom does not presume to teach, but only to explain what the teaching and the training envolves. For this reason it is not proposed to expound the other Laws and Principles, each with its application to the personality as the basis of ethics and character building, and each with its deeper application to the purpose of the soul in its struggle to evoke soul awareness in the personality for the purpose of service to the Plan at the physical level. The very names of these Laws and Principles are sufficient to provoke an understanding of their dual application;

> The Law of Right Human Relations
> The Law of Group Endeavour
> The Law of Spiritual Approach
> The Law of Cause and Effect
> The Law of Attraction
> The Principle of Goodwill
> The Principle of Essential Divinity
> The Principle of Unanimity

There are many more Laws and Principles of the Kingdom of God, as they are oftimes called when considered in the light of their application to the

The Seed of Wisdom

world of souls, which *is* the Kingdom of God. The names of most of them are descriptive enough for understanding of their general application, although perhaps the strange name – The Principle of Unanimity – requires explanation.

This Principle deals with the essential unity which underlies all creation, and is therefore of paramount interest and importance. We see all created things, including ourselves, as separate forms: and even as souls – when we have some degree of soul awareness – we feel we are separate units of consciousness. It is, as we have seen earlier, through this sense of separateness that the mind analyses and experiences everything in life. But eventually we have to start the process of synthesis, of putting together the pieces we have separated in our minds. We have also to start the work of integrating the three aspects of the personality into one coherent vehicle of expression, and then of fusing this integrated personality with the soul. Only then is it remotely possible to sense, except in theory, the underlying unity with all other souls, and to arrive at the realisation that all souls are but differentiations of the one Soul. This is a concept which, at our stage of evolution, is impossible to grasp, because to do so, the process of fusion and re-absorbtion by the Whole must be well on the way; and this for us is but a far distant vision. But even the vision and theoretical knowledge of the reality is of value, and in practical terms the Tibetan tells us:

Practical Application

Synthesis dictates the trend of all the evolutionary processes today. All is working towards larger unified blocks, towards amalgamations, international relationships, global planning, brotherhood, economic fusion, and free flow of commodities everywhere, interdependence, fellowship of faiths, movements based upon the welfare of humanity as a whole and which militate against division, separation and isolation. Little as people realise it, these concepts are relatively new factors in human consciousness.*

Such is the meaning of the Principle of Unanimity, and it is interesting to note that this was written at least 40 years ago. The trend towards synthesis can be seen quite clearly from any review of recent history. We have only to consider the birth of the U. S. S. R., the U. S. A., the Italian and Spanish States; and in more recent times The League of Nations, the United Nations, the European Economic Community, the Ecumenical Council, and so on. In the field of practical politics today, one would imagine that the ideal formulated in the Principle of Unanimity should help us in forming a view on such questions as the U. K. entry into the European Community.

---

*From study papers of the Group for Creative Meditation on the Laws and Principles of the Kingdom of God.

Conclusion

M A N H A S, since time immemorial, forged his way ahead in every field of human endeavour, thanks to his own inherent qualities of intelligence and perseverence, and because of the vision of those who have opened up the way ahead. When it comes to spiritual progress, we discover two additional factors which carry us along the path which leads unerringly towards the goal. One is the knowledge that we are not alone in our endeavour, and the other is our inherent sense of divinity.

There are of course many roads that we can take towards that distant goal; and in the initial stages of the journey much will depend on what appear to be accidental circumstances; such as where we were born, and therefore what religion we were taught in our youth; what sort of family background has influenced our early life, and what inspiration – if any – has ever come our way.

The Ageless Wisdom teaching prompts us to question whether all, or indeed any, of these factors are as accidental as they at first appear. Once we accept the reality of the soul as the real centre of

Conclusion

consciousness in man, and the personality and physical body as one of the many 'outer garments of the soul', we begin to realise that these apparently accidental features of our lives are, to an increasing extent in the long life of the soul, a deliberate choice. The vision is clear – to the soul – but the trouble is that for countless lives there is no registering of the vision in the brain.

But once the many futile and restless activities of the brain have been stilled, and the emotional nature has been brought somewhat under control, the purpose of the life as visioned by the soul can be sensed. We then discover that all roads lead to the Path of truly conscious spiritual endeavour, which means service to the Plan. And then comes understanding, wisdom, serenity – and much hard work.

A vast amount has been written, first in the orient and then more recently in the occident; and the same thread runs through it all; but no amount of intellectual effort will lead to enlightment without the aid of meditation, for there is indeed a field of knowledge and of wisdom which is beyond the comprehension of the intellect without the aid of the intuition. But the esotericist is often just an average man of intellectual ability whose thoughts are beginning to turn inwards to seek a fuller life of deeper meaning. He has to earn his living like everyone else, help to bring up a family and run a household, and at the end of the day of work and travel many of us are too tired to read for as long as we might wish. Yet if we were able to list all the novels that we have read over the period of our active working life, let alone the years after retirement, the list would, for many of us, be quite impressive – in terms of volume. So one way to acquire the habit of spiritual reading is to set aside for this purpose even half an hour each day. Most of the reading can be quite fascinating, and almost inevitably spiritual reading grows on us quite fast and soon takes the place of reading just to 'pass the time'. One book leads on to another and those which carry a school of thought or a philosophy of life become books of reference, to be read or re-read as the expansion of awareness enables us better to understand what at first seems obscure and difficult. It is important, in this connection, never to allow a difficult passage to block the way, because so often we find that by reading on, we acquire the intuitive sense to interpret its meaning. It has been said that, if just one new idea drops into the mind as a result of reading a book, it was worth reading it.

A list of the books of Alice A. Bailey, carrying the teaching of the Tibetan Master, Djwal Khul, which is the foundation of my own faith and conviction in these matters, is given in Appendix II, followed in Appendix III by a relatively short selection from the very great number of other books for further reading. *The Golden Thread* by Natalie N. Banks provides an excellent survey of the origin and continuity of the Ageless Wisdom teaching, in short and concise terms. The books of Raynor Johnson, starting with

Conclusion

The Imprisoned Splendour and ending with *The Situation of Modern Man* present the views of a scientist, beginning with a most cautious and agnostic approach, through the heightening conviction of the occultist, to the sensed knowing of the mystic. Of the A. A. B. books, I would particularly recommend *A Treatise on White Magic* (available in paper-back edition), despite the strange title which might put some people off. Magic is defined in Webster's dictionary as 'the pretended art of working by the power or assistance of supernatural beings'. But here there is no pretence, for I hope that this brief introduction to esotericism may lead to the conviction, or at least a theoretical realisation that man *can* work in the field of human evolution with the help of the Masters of the Wisdom. Magic in this context is working with mental matter, and becoming *aware* of the creation by the soul of thought-forms for us to materialise by action at the mental and physical level. The Tibetan tells us that:

> All work and all created thought-forms (whether they materialise as an organisation, a religion, a school of thought, a book or a life work of any kind) which express spiritual ideals and lay the emphasis upon the life aspect come under the category of white magic.

A Treatise on White Magic is widely based, not too

The Seed of Wisdom

difficult to follow, deeply spiritual, and at the same time practical.

The attainment of what D. K. refers to as the 'esoteric sense', earlier defined in this book as 'essentially the power to live and function subjectively, and to possess a constant inner contact with the soul and the world in which it is found', is high ambition indeed, but through spiritual reading and meditation a start can be made, resulting inevitably in the ability to look instinctively for the underlying causes of events and of the problems that arise in our own lives and in the world around us. In doing so we cannot fail to develop that subtle quality of understanding – of our personal faults and failures, without morbid introspection – as well as the difficulties with which others have to contend.

I would like to close with a final quotation from the writings of the Tibetan, infinitely more expressive than any words of my own could be, concerning the urgency for service in the world today, by a conscious and deliberate effort to develop the intuition.

Every human being who reaches the goal of light and wisdom automatically has a field of influence which extends both up and down, and which reaches both inwards to the source of light and outwards into 'the fields of darkness'. When he has thus attained he will become a conscious centre of life giving force, and will be so without effort. He will stimulate, energise and vivify to fresh efforts

Conclusion

all lives that he contacts, be they his fellow aspirants, or an animal or a flower. He will act as a transmitter of light. He will dispel the glamour around him and let in the radiance of reality.

When large numbers of the sons of men can so act, then the human family will enter upon its destined work of planetary service. Its mission is to act as a bridge between the world of spirit and the world of material forms. All grades of matter meet in man, and all the states of consciousness are possible to him. Mankind can work in all directions and lift the sub-human kingdoms into heaven and bring heaven down to earth.

The point to be grasped is that through humanity on the physical plane, the nature of reality will be revealed, the true and the beautiful will be manifested; the divine plan will eventually work out, and that energy be transmitted to all forms in nature which will enable the inner spiritual reality to emerge.

Such is the distant vision. But however distant it may appear, there is encouragement at every step along the path towards a deeper understanding of the inner meaning of life. I hope that this brief introduction to the teaching of the Ageless Wisdom may be of some help to those who, like myself, are searching for the nature of reality.

APPENDIX I
EXTRACT FROM A STATEMENT BY THE TIBETAN

I am a brother of yours, who has travelled a little longer upon the Path than has the average student, and has therefore incurred greater responsibilities. I am one who has wrestled and fought his way into a greater measure of light than has the aspirant who will read this article, and I must therefore act as a transmitter of the light, at no matter what cost. My work is to teach and spread the knowledge of the Ageless Wisdom wherever I can find a response, and I have been doing this for many years. I seek also to help the Master M. and the Master K.H. whenever opportunity offers, for I have been long connected with Them and with Their work. In all the above, I have told you much; yet at the same time I have told you nothing which would lead you to offer me that blind obedience and the foolish devotion which the emotional aspirant offers to the Guru and Master whom he is as yet unable to contact. Nor will he make that desired contact until he has transmuted emotional devotion into unselfish service to humanity — not to the Master.

The books that I have written are sent out with no claim for their acceptance. They may, or may not, be correct, true and useful. It is for you to ascertain their truth by right practice and by the exercise of the intuition. Neither I nor

Appendixes

A. A. B. is the least interested in having them acclaimed as inspired writings, or in having anyone speak of them (with bated breath) as being the work of one of the Masters. If they present truth in such a way that it follows sequentially upon that already offered in the world teachings, if the information given raises the aspiration and the will-to-serve from the plane of the emotions to that of the mind (the plane whereon the Masters can be found) then they will have served their purpose. If the teaching conveyed calls forth a response from the illumined mind of the worker in the world, and brings a flashing forth of his intuition, then let that teaching be accepted. But not otherwise. If the statements meet with eventual corroboration, or are deemed true under the test of the Law of Correspondences, then that is well and good. But should this not be so, let not the student accept what is said.

August 1934

APPENDIX II

BOOKS BY ALICE A. BAILEY

Initiation, Human and Solar
Letters on Occult Meditation
The Consciousness of the Atom
A Treatise on Cosmic Fire
The Light of the Soul
The Soul and Its Mechanism
From Intellect to Intuition
A Treatise on White Magic
From Bethlehem to Calvary
Discipleship in the New Age – Vol. I
Discipleship in the New Age – Vol. II
The Problems of Humanity
The Reappearance of the Christ
The Destiny of the Nations
Glamour : A World Problem
Telepathy and the Etheric Vehicle
The Unfinished Autobiography
Education in the New Age
The Externalisation of the Hierarchy
A Treatise on the Seven Rays :
VOL. I Esoteric Psychology
VOL. II Esoteric Psychology

Appendixes

VOL. III Esoteric Astrology
VOL. IV Esoteric Healing
VOL. V The Rays and the Initiations

Published by
LUCIS PUBLISHING COMPANY
New York
&
LUCIS PRESS LTD
London

APPENDIX III

OTHER BOOKS SUGGESTED FOR READING

The Astral Body, Lt-Col. A. E. Powell, Theosophical Publishing House, London.

Breakthrough to Creativity, Shafica Karagulla, M. D., de Vorss & Co., Santa Monica, California.

The Imprisoned Splendour, Raynor C. Johnson, Hodder & Stoughton, London.

In Search of the Miraculous, P. D. Ouspensky, Routledge & Kegan Paul, London.

The Candle of Vision, 'A.E.'

The Causal Body and the Ego, Lt-Col. A. E. Powell, Theosophical Publishing House, London.

Changing Esoteric Values, Foster Bailey, Lucis Press, London.

The Christian Agnostic, Dr. Leslie D. Weatherhead, Hodder and Stoughton, London.

Concentration, Ernest Wood, Theosophical Publishing House, London.

Concerning the Inner Life, Evelyn Underhill.

Cosmic Consciousness, Maurice Bucke, Dutton and Co., New York.

Eastern Religions and Western Thought, S. Radhakrishnan, Clarenden Press, Oxford.

Appendixes

The Golden Thread, Natalie N. Banks, Lucis Press, London.

The Etheric Double, Lt-Col. A. E. Powell, Theosophical Publishing House, London.

The Expansion of Awareness, Arthur W. Osborn, The Omega Press, Reigate, Surrey.

The Light and the Gate, Raynor C. Johnson, Hodder and Stoughton, London.

Man, the Measure of All Things, Sri Krishna Prem and Sri Madhava Ashish, Rider and Co., London.

Man Visible and Invisible, C. W. Leadbetter.

The Mental Body, Lt-Col. A. E. Powell, Theosophical Publishing House, London.

Modern Man in Search of a Soul, C. G. Jung.

The Mystical Ladder, John Sinclair, Spiritualist Association of Great Britain, London.

A New Model of the Universe, P. D. Ouspensky, Routledge & Kegan Paul, London.

Nurslings of Immortality, Raynor C. Johnson, Hodder & Stoughton, London.

The Open Way, E. Graham Howe & L. Le Mesurier, John Watkins, London.

Pointing the Way, Martin Buber, Routledge & Kegan Paul, London.

The Perennial Philosophy, Aldous Huxley, Chatto and Windus.

Practical Mysticism, Evelyn Underhill, J. M. Dent & Sons.

The Inner Reality, Paul Brunton, Rider and Co., London.

The Psychology of Man's Possible Evolution, P. D. Ouspensky, Hodder and Stoughton, London.

The Seed of Wisdom

Psychosynthesis, Dr. Robert Assagioli, Hobbs, Dorman and Co., New York.

The Psychology of Man's Possible Evolution, P. D. Ouspensky, Hodder & Stoughton, London.

Rajah Yoga, Swami Vivekananda.

The Secret Doctrine, Vols. I, II, III, H. P. Blavatsky, Theosophical Publishing Society.

The Secret Path, Paul Brunton, Rider and Co., London.

Sidhartha, Herman Hesse, Peter Owen Vision Press, London.

The Silent Path, Michal Eastcott, Rider and Co., London.

The Situation of Modern Man, Raynor C. Johnson, A.R.E. Press, Virginia.

Tertium Organum, P. D. Ouspensky, Routledge & Kegan Paul, London.

The Upanishads, Translations with Foreword by Juan Mascaró, Penguin Books Ltd.

Watcher on the Hills, Raynor C. Johnson, Hodder & Stoughton, London.

The Yoga of the Bhagavad Gita, Shri Krishna Prem, John Watkins, London.

The Axis and the Rim, Arthur W. Osborn, The Omega Press, Reigate, Surrey.

Fruits of Silence, Hugh l'Anson Fausset, John M. Watkins, London.